Alternatives to Custody

edited by

JOHN POINTING

Basil Blackwell

© Basil Blackwell Ltd 1986

First published 1986

Basil Blackwell Ltd
108 Cowley Road, Oxford OX4 1JF, UK

Basil Blackwell Inc.
432 Park Avenue South, Suite 1503,
New York, NY 10016, USA

British Library Cataloguing in Publication Data

Alternatives to custody.
1. Corrections—Great Britain
I. Pointing, John
364.6'8'0941   HV9345.A5

ISBN 0-631-14701-2
ISBN 0-631-14702-0 Pbk

Library of Congress Cataloging in Publication Data

Main entry under title:

Alternatives to custody.

Bibliography: p.
Includes index.
1. Probation—Great Britain. 2. Rehabilitation of
criminals—Great Britain. I. Pointing, John.
HV9345.A5A48 1986   364.6'3'0941   85-22979
ISBN 0-631-14701-2
ISBN 0-631-14702-0 (pbk.)

Typeset by Photo·Graphics, Honiton, Devon
Printed in Great Britain by The Bath Press, Avon

Contents

Preface

The idea of writing a book on alternatives to custody arose from a conversation between Richard Hil and myself one rainy day during the spring of 1982. At that time we were employed as researchers in the probation service and were equally frustrated by the inability of those in positions of authority to take research seriously. We were only partly frustrated by the marginalization of our work afforded by those managing a public bureaucracy. The other part stemmed from the knowledge that the world outside the probation service had little or no idea of what probation was about. The book grew from this as we found that other researchers and practitioners were finding their work ignored, misunderstood, and even denigrated by those in positions of authority. Although innovatory projects and methods of working had their advocates, it was clear that there was no coherent policy on development in the probation service. It also became apparent that there was little appreciation of the desirability for the probation service to promote the development of alternatives to custody. To us there seemed to be an irony in that the 'institutional inarticulateness' we found coincided with a crisis point in the state of British prisons. A pragmatic need to develop alternatives to custody seemed so obvious, and we could not entirely understand why the probation service had been unsuccessful in projecting credible alternatives to a wider public.

It is clearer to me now than it was in 1982 that the probation service bears some responsibility for this situation continuing, but not sole responsibility. It is my view, and that of others, that we need to engage in a 'moral crusade' against the use and abuse of imprisonment as a sentence of the courts. We need to sustain a moral crusade to allow time for a radical transformation of the criminal justice system to take place. Moreover, it is necessary that many people and institutions throughout society be involved in such a crusade, and I am indebted to Andrew Rutherford for making this point clear to me.

Our contribution to this process in the form of this book is a modest one. We have aimed to open up an area of work in probation in order to facilitate debate, and bring forward the time of institutional change. We think there are lessons to be learned from our experience and hope that the quality of future developments may improve as a result. We have been conscious of the importance of maintaining a balanced assessment of our material, and accept that there will be instances where this may not have been successful. In the end, each reader has to decide on this for himself or herself. It should be clear to our readers that this book does not have the official backing of any public agency: the views expressed are those of the particular author of each chapter. The responsibility for the overall shape of the book lies with me.

The sources we have drawn upon in preparing *Alternatives to Custody* are very wide. In particular, we are indebted to the cooperation of hundreds of probation clients. Conversations and interviews with dozens of probation officers and managers form another empirical base of the book. It would be both impractical and invidious to single out individuals from either of these groups, but without their participation and cooperation the book could not have been written. Various people have made helpful criticisms of the text. These have all been taken into account, though possibly not as much as some commentators would have liked.

The early stages of preparing *Alternatives to Custody* were undertaken jointly by Richard Hil and myself. Richard had to bow out of sharing the burden of editing because of other commitments. I owe him a very real debt for sharing the initial work. I know I would not have thought of the project alone: it originated from an idea we formulated together.

London   J.P.

1

Introduction

John Pointing

The provision and development of alternatives to custody provide the focus for this collection of essays. 'Alternatives' is used in the title of this book in order to emphasize that penal policy results from choices and conscious decisions made by policy makers. This is not to deny the difficulty of making changes in policy, but to argue that the practice of penal policy cannot be satisfactorily explained in terms of resistance to change and innovation within existing institutions. We stress the element of choice because, put simply, society can either continue to send increasing numbers of people to prison, or alternative cheaper and better arrangements for dealing with offenders can be established in the community. We believe that the latter choice is preferable, particularly with regard to petty offenders and young people who together make up a substantial proportion of the prison population. The programmes discussed in this book apply with regard to offenders committing frequent but relatively minor offences, and we are not making a case for releasing into the community serious offenders convicted of major property crimes or serious crimes of violence.

The diversion of offenders from the prison system (which includes detention centres and youth custody centres) is, on the surface, widely supported. It must be appreciated, however, that support for prisons constitutes a deeply-held emotional force for some people and is by no means a simple reaction to

societal deviance and deviation. The demand to make offenders pay for misdeeds, the desire to deter potential offenders,
and the provision of a salutary reminder to everyone about the
authority of 'the State' possess an emotional and moral
dimension of great power (McConville, 1981). Prisons constitute both the symbolic core of the criminal justice system,
and, more prosaically, they provide the places where people
end up if they are caught often enough for committing trivial
offences. Alternatives to prison cannot hope to compete on the
emotional/moral front; they tend not to be viewed as equivalent to prison, being seen instead as 'soft options'. This means
that it is very difficult indeed for criminal justice policy to
change from having a custodial focus towards which an
increasing proportion of offenders are drawn over time.

In view of the emotional/moral dimension to prison, official
statements of support for non-custodial alternatives must be
treated with caution. Furthermore there is often considerable
confusion underlying such support. Organizations such as the
probation service are uncomfortable about recognizing the
role of punishment in the criminal justice system, and probation officers often refuse to accept their role as being based on
the exercise of social control (cf. Griffiths, 1982b; Lacey et al.
1983). This poses a problem since it means that custodial
alternatives are almost apologized for, and may not be seen
and used as direct alternatives. Moreover, they are sometimes
treated with suspicion amongst professional colleagues (cf.
Hil, 1980). Social workers' apologetics can thus be seen as a
reflection of the emotional/moral dimension underpinning
penal policy: a dimension that has been historically fuelled by
the 'law-and-order' lobby.

Geoffrey Pearson has commented on these issues in terms of
a broad historical perspective. Pearson shows that a 'law-and-
order' movement is as powerful today as in previous genera-
tions, and the fact that 'myths' pervade arguments about
crime does not detract from that power:

We are dealing with a form of moral dodo-ism, marked by its
inability to keep pace with a moving world and to adapt its

complaints to sometimes dramatic social alterations. But it is an unusually lively dodo: one that keeps escaping from the museum, and which is currently on the rampage in the vigorous shape of the 'law-and-order' movement. It is therefore not enough to shrug off these fears and doom fantasies as mothball reaction, or to say that they signify nothing. Because, while we might wish to redress the historical dimension, crime and violence are indisputably immediate social realities; and the fears which circulate around the criminal question are a potent cultural and political force. (Pearson, 1983, 211)

Part of the problem of establishing alternatives to prison is that these require rational arguments and cannot rely on the emotional and moral discourse which underpins prisons. Prisons do not have to deliver positive benefits, and even the Home Office now defines prisons in terms of their providing 'humane containment' (Guardian, 24 February, 1983). We might well question the 'humane' part of this description, particularly since it has been made in the context of the Chief Inspector of Prisons report dealing with overcrowding. The Chief Inspector found that conditions in many prisons were 'unacceptable', but did not question the existence of or 'need' for prisons (Home Office, 1981d). The choice for the Chief Inspector lies between expanding the number of available places through a more active building programme and reducing the prison population to manageable proportions through early release for petty offenders, namely a 12½ per cent reduction to 37,000. He supports the latter as a short-term expedient to fulfil the aim of 'humane containment' and to buy time for the 'necessary' building programme to take place. Underlying the position of the prisons inspectorate is a firm commitment to the continued use of prisons as a deterrent to offenders and as a method of dealing with 'serious offenders'. Though critical of many elements of penal practice, the inspectorate is in accord with the Home Office regarding the pivotal role of custodial institutions in dealing with crime.

This, however, has not prevented senior civil servants from commenting on the state of prisons. For example, in commenting upon Strangeways' policy of locking up young prisoners and Borstal trainees for 23 hours per day, the Deputy Inspector of Prisons described their consequent lifestyle as 'barren', adding that: 'for this age group, the absence of education and work for all but a minority, and the consequent restriction to the cell for up to 23 hours a day, is particularly to be regretted' (*Guardian*, 22 April 1983).

The Home Office justifies its failure to confront the prisons crisis – which for them is only a crisis of overcrowding – by claiming political and 'public' support for implementing custodial sanctions. From the Home Office point of view, present policy protects the public and public money is wisely spent in keeping crime off the streets. Whether such aims are achieved is highly questionable, but a further issue is raised; namely, how far does the 'public' support punitive and custodial measures in dealing with crime? Judges, politicians, top policemen and the popular media all claim to act as the surrogate mind of the public, and the conventional wisdom is that the public supports a 'tough' policy for offenders and is quite prepared to pay for it in the shape of prisons. Tom Mangold's comments about fellow journalists' capacities to reflect public opinion seem equally applicable to politicians and Home Office mandarins: 'After 30 years in mass communications I fear I still would not know public opinion if it bit me in the behind; just do not tell me that some Fleet Street leader writer staggering out of El Vino's at four in the afternoon represents public opinion' (*Listener*, 25 February 1982).

Recent studies indicate that the public response to crime may not be to call for increasingly punitive and custodial sanctions. Stephen Shaw, the Director of the Prison Reform Trust, found from his research that: 'two-thirds of the British people would support an amnesty for persons convicted of minor offences' (*The Times*, 20 September 1982). This support tends to correspond with views held by some members of the liberal establishment. Thus Lord Hunt has called for: 'automatic, conditional release under supervision for all prisoners serving 18 months imprisonment, or less' (*The Times*, 1 December 1981). Such arguments are as relevant to the immediate problem of overcrowding as to the diversion of a substantial proportion of the prison population from custody.

Firmer evidence for a more liberal climate of opinion than is currently supposed is contained in the first *British Crime Survey*. This imaginative and wide-ranging Home Office survey of a large, nationally representative sample of victims found that:

Only half (of victims) felt that if caught 'their' offender(s) should be brought before the courts. 10% of victims favoured a prison or borstal sentence; the figure rose for victims of burglary and car theft to 36% and 31% respectively. Perhaps surprisingly, only 2% of victims proposed judicial corporal punishment. The most favoured sanction (mentioned by a quarter of victims) was a fine; a fifth wanted a formal caution from the police or some sort of less formal reprimand; 15% mentioned some form of reparation, either community service or direct compensation by the offender. 12% felt that no action was called for at all. (Hough and Mayhew, 1983, 28)

This evidence suggests that there is substantially less support for punitive and custodial sentences than has been assumed hitherto by many politicians, judges and civil servants. It is possible, moreover, that the spurious consensus militating for the continued over-use of custody is in serious disarray. Thus two Conservative members of the influential All-Party Penal Affairs Group have recently expressed unequivocal opposition to current penal policy.

First, Charles Irving argued that:

It would need only a tiny fraction of the money devoted to prison building, at a capital cost of nearly £50,000 per new prison place, to provide more humane and cost-effective alternatives for many non-violent offenders and for the more than 20,000 fine defaulters who are imprisoned each year. Alternatives to prison not only make humanitarian and penological sense, they also make economic sense. (*Guardian*, 20 July 1983)

Second, Janet Fookes argued that the prisons crisis was not simply one of overcrowding, but also resulted from the over-use of prisons in dealing with crime: 'We use imprisonment far more than other nations of Western Europe, whose experience suggests that the lengths of sentences served by many non-violent offenders could be reduced without endangering the public' (*Guardian*, 20 July 1983).

It is possible, therefore, that there is wider public support for the view that the prisons crisis is not simply one of overcrowding, and a more important issue is therefore raised; namely, what are prisons for? Mr John McCarthy's answer that prisons are dustbins for dealing with social failures and for hiding society's failures was echoed in a subsequent *Guardian* editorial of 2 June 1982: 'Our prisons are the dustbins for intractable social problems. They are the end of the line, they cannot turn away people sent to them by the courts. So they house a variety of inadequates and social catastrophes who fall through the large holes in the health and welfare system – vagrants, alcoholics, mentally disturbed people.' Mr Ian Dunbar – Mr McCarthy's successor as Governor of Wormwood Scrubs – has also been equally critical of present Home Office policy. In a National Association for the Care and Resettlement of Offenders (NACRO) lecture, he judiciously avoided breaking the Official Secrets Act in stating: 'A body blow to those of us who believe prisons should exist only if they can achieve a positive purpose by stopping people becoming serious criminals is the general conclusion that, with few exceptions, all custodial programmes are equally ineffective in preventing re-offending' (*Guardian*, 14 January 1983).

The case for diverting offenders from prison rests on the over-use of custodial facilities such that a significant proportion of inmates, being petty persistent offenders, have become entangled in a 'revolving door' relationship to prison (Willis, chapter 2 below). Home Office (1981c) statistics demonstrate that over 50 per cent of the 1980 prison population was made up of offenders committing property crimes of burglary, theft, and taking and driving away (TDA). A decarceration policy, aimed at setting up community-based alternatives to prison, need divert only a fraction of this population and would still make substantial inroads into custody figures.

Evidence for the routine but trivial nature of the bulk of property offences is provided by the *British Crime Survey*. The researchers found that only 22 per cent of attempted or successful burglaries – offences for which a custodial outcome is most likely for offenders over 17 – resulted in losses of over £100 (Hough and Mayhew, 1983, 18). With regard to theft, the researchers found that the majority of incidents (excluding theft of vehicles) were not even reported to the police (Hough and Mayhew, 1983, 11). Although many victims had doubts about the efficacy of the police as a crime-solving agency, the main reason for non-reporting was because the offences in question were considered to be too trivial to be worth reporting.

A major irony of the criminal justice system is that what is intended as liberal legislation, for example the 1969 Children and Young Persons' Act, results in practice in the greater use of custody (cf. Morris et al., 1980; Taylor et al., 1980; Thorpe et al., 1980). This is partly because the actual development of non-custodial alternatives has lagged severely behind the progress anticipated to result from such legislation. Social services departments and the probation service have been unable to initiate a sufficient range of alternatives: partly through inability to get sufficient funds, partly through their lack of skill in setting up projects, and partly through simple bureaucratic inertia. Nevertheless the key to the development of alternatives lies in sentencing practice, and sentencers in the main behave in a punitive manner. The increasingly punitive trend to sentencing is reversible, and after all there is no rational basis or 'need' for it. It is an intention of this book to offer practical alternatives to custody for those convicted of petty crimes who, nevertheless, find themselves being sent to prison establishments. Committal to custody is not only seen as an inappropriate response to petty offending, but also as

harmful on public policy grounds, since many more petty
offenders are likely to become trapped in a 'revolving door'
relationship to prison unless there is significant development
of alternative programmes (Willis, chapter 2 below).

It is important to bear in mind that if custodial facilities are
provided and expanded, as has occurred in the wake of the
1982 Criminal Justice Act, then the number of offenders sent
to prison, youth custody and detention centres will undoubtedly increase. This Act provides the foundations for enhancing
the increasingly punitive trend in sentencing. It raises the
prospect of larger numbers of young offenders going into
custody, since no effective controls on the powers of magistrates to send young people to detention centres or prisons have
been introduced. However, the Act also provides some
support for community-based alternatives to custody and en-
courages a widening of the sentencing tariff for young people. This
requires imagination and the utilization of new management
skills by social work agencies, both in developing new
programmes and in influencing magistrates' sentencing practices. Unfortunately the effectiveness of such developments is
likely to be patchy, and there can be little confidence of
reversing the trend – at the national level – towards the
increasing use of custody unless major new resources are made
available and social work agencies develop a much more
positive approach to the development of custodial alternatives.

To summarize, the main concerns of this book are to
demonstrate, first, that major changes are required in the use
of resources dealing with offenders, and second, that there are
already available non-custodial schemes and programmes for
offenders which could be developed on a wider basis. We
argue further that the provision and development of custodial
alternatives and the decreased dependence on prisons must be
seen as part of the same process. Although alternatives to
custody have long been available to sentencers, these have had
little influence in reducing the prison population. The size of
the prison population is largely determined by sentencers'
decisions, and particularly magistrates' decisions in view of

the large numbers of petty offenders sent to custody for shorter terms. The crux of the problem is that whereas sentencers need to have a greater range of sentencing options in the field of alternatives to custody, their powers to impose custodial sentences, and particularly long sentences, also need to be sharply curtailed.

The need for such changes is not accepted by the present government, but then neither are much more modest attempts to set up a coordinating machinery between sentencers and other agencies. The immediate prospects for greater coordination are not encouraging, and the government's preparedness to support inter-agency consultation is no substitute for change. To quote Stephen Shaw (*Guardian*, 15 August 1983): 'What strikes one is the basic ad hocery which characterises the present arrangements. There is also all the difference in the world between *consultation* among related services and the *planning* of what is inevitably an interdependent system as a whole.'

The contributions in this book share a modesty about the potential of non-custodial programmes to stop people reoffending. This will come as no surprise to people working with offenders since there is no single solution to the problem posed by repeated offending. This is because crime is a firmly entrenched feature of society. The ubiquitous nature of crime means that policy has to be geared to managing crime and its effects and in pursuing a strategy of containment. To continue pretending that crime is an individual phenomenon which can be solved by means of heavy sentencing or by pursuing any particular social work panacea is to engage in the politics of fantasy. It remains, however, a pervasive fantasy, shared by policy makers both in national and local government and by social work managers.

Although the programmes described in this book may only provide the most modest grounds for securing longer-term benefits in terms of offending patterns, they are all reasonably successful in containing offending during the time people attend them. Programme objectives tend to be wider than the prevention of reoffending because they are geared to the actual problems which face people attending programmes: problems which may act either as underlying or contributory causes of offending. Objectives are diverse also because the programmes address themselves to various groups of offenders, and it cannot be stressed too much that the further development of non-custodial programmes has to recognize and act in accordance with such diversity.

In their separate ways the essays in this book confront the problem of developing social work methods in order to supervise offenders in the community. This poses many problems at the field level, since innovatory programmes are often contentious within social work organizations. Conflict within these organizations is often not properly resolved and, in particular, managers are often ambivalent about innovation, and insufficiently trained and skilled at project development. However, the main concern of this introduction is with the national level of policy making, and the implications regarding social work's delivery of alternatives are considered by Ian Butler in the concluding chapter.

The policy issues which need to be debated, developed and pursued in the 1980s, if alternatives to custody are to become a substantial part of the criminal justice system instead of merely amounting to a gestural sop to liberals, can be summarized as follows. First, sentencers need to have confidence in custodial alternatives if they are to be used more often and for a wider range of offenders. The onus must rest on the statutory social work organizations for the development of such alternatives, but the role of the voluntary sector, and community organizations in particular, is crucial in facilitating development. Second, radical changes in the way in which social work bureaucracies operate and are managed are essential, and follow from the above point. Moreover, social work itself – both in its practice and theory – needs to develop a far more sophisticated understanding of the social and structural contexts of clients' problems. Central to this is understanding from the clients' point of view: an understanding which is seriously hindered by the 'hierarchy of credibility' inherent in bureaucratic organizations (cf. Becker, 1967, 241). Third, the criminal justice system itself requires reorganization as a system, at both local and national levels, as opposed to what it is at present, namely an *ad hoc* collection of traditional practices to which new layers are added, and which is held together by largely untested assumptions about the nature of offending. It then becomes possible to organize a substantial and phased run-down of custodial facilities, leading to the closure of detention centres and prisons, at the same time as new, non-custodial facilities are set up and become established. Furthermore, new institutional arrangements are needed for diverting particular groups of offenders, particularly younger offenders, from court disposals. Extending the use of police cautioning, extending the scope and powers of juvenile liaison bureaux and increasing the gatekeeping role of social work agencies all seem essential in this.

A campaign against the continuing over-use of custodial facilities is only useful if alternatives to custody form an integral part of it. This collection of essays makes a contribution to such a campaign. Indeed, all the contributions are based on projects which deal with 'difficult' groups of offenders, at least as defined from the point of view of social work agencies. However, perhaps the most important point to make about the essays presented in this book is their diversity, both with regard to the programmes themselves and to the groups of people attending them. Important though a recognition of diversity is for the development of custodial alternatives, it also makes it difficult and perhaps presumptuous to make too many generalizations about them.

However, there has been a systematic attempt made in all the contributions to elicit the clients' point of view. Many of the contributors try to use the clients' views as a basis for comparison with the perceptions and practices of the staff running programmes. We think the importance of this is two-fold. First of all, the clients' point of view has generally been ignored in the development of social work services for offenders. Second, a way of encouraging the development of workable programmes is to match clients' definitions with social workers' definitions. By doing this, social work practice can be systematically evaluated and changes brought about in ways that are helpful to offenders. These issues, which stem directly from Bottoms' and McWilliams' 'paradigm of help' (1979), are discussed further in several of the contributions.

Although it is not possible to distil theoretical coherence from this collection of essays, there would seem to be four principal ingredients that alternatives to custody need to offer or encourage. First, controls on clients' behaviour need to be built into programmes if they are going to be seen by magistrates as offering 'real' alternatives to custody. Second, the community has to benefit, both in terms of cost and in terms of the programme effecting a pay-back from offenders to the community from which they are drawn. Third, offenders need to be able to acquire new skills and experiences for diversion from offending patterns of behaviour to be possible. Finally, much more supportive community facilities and responsive statutory agencies are needed for clients once they complete programmes.

Turning to the individual contributions in this book, these are divided into two basic categories. The first deals with direct alternatives to custody for offenders who, at the time of entry to the project, have not usually had previous custodial experience, but who probably would have had without the custodial alternative. Chapter 3 by Peter Murray on the controversial Medway Close Support Unit, and chapter 4 by Peter Harraway on the Driver Retraining Scheme are projects of this type.

The Close Support Unit (CSU) is important since it has constituted a pioneering attempt to replace committal to detention centres by a form of intensive, community-based supervision. It raises the problem that clients who offend after their attendance at the unit are more than likely to end up in residential 'care' or detention centres. It is controversial largely because of the fears within the probation service that it makes officers adopt a punitive approach towards offenders. It is an important scheme despite these shortcomings, since the unit pioneered a form of intensive intermediate treatment (IT) supported by the Department of Health and Social Security (DHSS), which currently attracts government funding arising from a recent Circular: LAC (83)3.

The Driver Retraining Scheme is a very different project in the sense that it works with a selected group of offenders having histories of driving offences, notably TDA. Similarly intended as a direct alternative to custody, this project bases probation intervention on a programme designed to open up channels for legitimate driving. The scheme not only demonstrates that offenders can learn new skills serving to help them avoid committing fresh offences, but also that such benefits apply to the period after completing their probation orders.

The second main category of contributions concerns projects intended mainly for people with custodial experience. These are diversionary projects, of varying degrees of intensity, which are intended to help people change their ways of life to avoid subsequent offending and probable punitive sentencing. Such projects are more frequently found in the probation service, partly because they fit in better with that service's tradition of prison after-care, and partly because the provision of direct alternatives to custody remains controversial in the probation service. Chapters 5 to 9, inclusive, fall into this category.

Chapter 5 on the Southampton Day Centre (by Richard Hil) and chapter 6 on the Pontypridd Day Training Centre (by Maurice Vanstone) are projects providing day-care support for clients. Both contributors highlight the need for social workers to be innovative and flexible in organizing activities, and stress the importance of basing programmes on problems as perceived by clients. Hil's chapter is particularly revealing in that it charts the controversy surrounding probation supervision in the community, and highlights the often conflicting perspectives of field workers and managers. Vanstone stresses that the key problems for clients –

unemployment and shortage of money – are not amenable to solution by social work action, though social workers can offer considerable help with lower (but no less important) priorities.

Vanstone's position, which points to the need for wider socio-economic changes to resolve clients' key problems, is further supported by John Pointing's analysis of supported work. Pointing's paper shows that whereas most clients possess apparently ordinary attitudes to work and unemployment, even such intensive schemes as 'Bulldog' can do very little to solve clients' employment problems. Pointing argues that the assumptions behind supported-work programmes are redundant in a depressed economy, and calls for a much more imaginative approach enabling clients to find alternatives to conventional forms of work.

Helen Bethune's chapter on the Alcoholics Recovery Project (ARP), like those on Bulldog and the Driver Retraining Scheme, considers the situation of offenders with a specifically identified problem. Bethune bases discussion on the enormous difficulties that need to be faced in social work if people suffering from alcoholism are to be helped. She also examines the implications raised when alcoholics do not recognize their problems in terms of alcohol abuse. This paper highlights the dilemma posed by all alternatives to custody, namely that if programmes are not available early enough in a delinquent or deviant career then the effectiveness of intervention is questionable since it is often too late to effect change.

The appropriateness of adventure activities for offenders with personality disorders and relatively extensive criminal histories is advocated in chapter 9, by Pat Maitland. This is an interesting conclusion since adventure activities are normally provided for young people 'at risk' of offending or for minor offenders rather than the people in Maitland's study. Maitland shows that occasional programmes are useful for her group of clients as a supplement to probation supervision, and her paper differs from others mentioned so far which are all based on formally set up alternatives.

Willis's second paper on probation officer/client interaction (chapter 10) reassesses conventional probation intervention, and is not based on an actual project. It is an important paper on both theoretical and practical grounds, since it provides a test of Bottoms' and McWilliams' 'paradigm of help' (1979). Willis's conclusion that the provision of practical help by officers is far more significant than the exercise of direct control or provision of psychodynamic casework will be encouraging to many field probation officers and managers.

The final chapter, by Ian Butler, provides an overview of the contributions from the viewpoint of a field social worker. This serves as a useful corrective to any over-identification that researchers might have had with the project they researched.

Alternatives to Custody is both a challenge to the prisons crisis and the product of a longstanding debate in social work about the relative merits of 'help' and 'treatment'. In varying degrees, all the contributions have been influenced by Bottoms' and McWilliams' (1979) analysis, though many of the programmes considered anticipated the ideas expressed in their paper. Bottoms and McWilliams argue that pathological explanations of offending are redundant, and should be replaced by explanations which stress clients' capabilities of making informed choices and decisions. The 'treatment' and 'help' models are contrasted as follows:

The treatment model, in its pure form, begins with a diagnosis by the caseworker of the clients' malfunctioning; then the treater decides upon the appropriate treatment with little or no advice from the client. The client is not offered choices about the form of appropriate treatment; he is assumed to be dependent and in need of expert attention. In the 'help' model, all this is radically transformed. The caseworker does not begin with an assumption of client malfunctioning; rather, he offers his unconditional help with client-defined tasks, this offer having certain definite and defined boundaries ... If the offer is accepted, this leads to a collaborative effort between worker and client to define the problem requiring help. (Bottoms and McWilliams, 1979, 172).

The position of the 'help' model with respect to alternatives
to custody also serves to explain why the diversity of provision
is unavoidable: the needs of offenders are various and their
situations in relation to patterns of offending are variable.
Moreover the flexibility of the provision of services for
offenders emanating from the probation order contrasts sharply with the uniformity of penal provision, in which 'humane
containment' is becoming the prime official objective.

The probation service as an institution has developed in
order to establish alternatives to custody, and to do this,
programmes at varying levels of intensity, purpose and content are needed. This may be unsatisfactory to those wanting
to see the establishment of a criminal justice system with
logical coherence and consistency. But it has to be admitted
that the variable nature of probation and social work acts as a
source of weakness, which is reflected in these essays on the
options available when viewed collectively. The situation
produced by conditions of variability results in uncertainty
and risk, which thereby generate failure if modest successes
occur also. There are risks inherent too in the development of
alternatives to custody which do not apply to carceral regimes,
since prisons are not judged on their effectiveness, and their
protagonists and staff no longer aspire to reform or rehabilitate
offenders.

It is in recognition of the difficult path trodden by alternatives to custody that this collection includes programmes
which have failed in some way, notably the chapters on
Bulldog, the Southampton Day Centre and the Medway Close
Support Unit. By publishing them, it is intended that mis-
takes will be more likely avoided in the future, but we would
also argue that errors are a feature of innovation. Furthermore
the failure of a programme may be largely the result of
external factors. Thus schemes trying to tackle unemployment
or alcoholism amongst serious offenders are almost doomed to
fail in important respects for many of their clients, no matter
how well formulated the planning, project development or
quality of the programme may be. Some problems are not

amenable to solution because of wider and structural socio-economic factors; this is not an argument for ignoring them but it should keep us searching for new ways of ameliorating them. Finally, the failure of programmes points towards a wider responsibility than that resting on social workers and their employing organizations: it lies with the whole society, including clients. An understanding of this may help to change Martin Davies's observation that: 'to go to a social work agency voluntarily is a sign of having "given up", to be compelled to go there is a mark, not only of failure, but of shame' (1981, 35).

The present prisons crisis requires that risks are taken, lessons are learned from failures and that gains are consolidated. The progress of alternatives to custody will not be an unproblematic ascent towards the rational and effective management of offending behaviour. This book is intended, therefore, to spur on social work agencies to continue making efforts in developing alternatives and, no less important, to give the rest of society a better idea of the nature of the problem.

2

Alternatives to Imprisonment: An Elusive Paradise?

Andrew Willis

At no other time in British penal history has the use of imprisonment been under such sustained criticism. The time is ripe, so it would seem, for a major penal initiative to promote non-custodial alternatives. This chapter examines some of the variables which constrain such developments, concluding that alternatives to custody, or community corrections, are an elusive but not impossible penal ambition.

Towards community corrections

The contemporary reality of imprisonment in England and Wales is grim: fortress-like buildings from a bygone age doing a job far in excess of what was ever intended. At any one time, nearly half of the 46,000 average daily population is crammed into just 24 local prisons, mostly dating from the period 1840–60, which were only ever intended to cater for around 11,000 prisoners. These ancient local gaols, then, are anything up to 100 per cent overcrowded. This generates quite appalling penal conditions for staff and inmates alike (Fitzgerald and Sim, 1979; Evans, 1980; King and Morgan, 1980; Willis, 1981b). It comes as no surprise, therefore, that the Director General of the Prison Department speaks repeatedly of crisis management because of chronic overcrowding and of conditions which are an affront to a civilized society (Home Office,

1981e, 1982b); or that a senior prison governor should speak out against his task which he likened to managing over-crowded cattle pens, and the purposeless warehousing of offenders in a large penal dustbin (*The Times*, 19 November 1981).

All this is now well known. There is, however, an even greater problem. It is concerned with the over-use and in-appropriate use of custody, and not just the lack of accom-modation in the Prison Department's Victorian inheritance. Home Office surveys, for example, find that as many as one-third of the average daily prison population could be regarded as minor or petty offenders whose criminality is much more of a social nuisance than threat; that some 20 per cent of them suffer from severe or gross mental disorder; and that one-in-three are without homes or roots in the community (Home Office, 1978a; Fairhead and Marshall, 1979; Fairhead, 1981b). These data point towards a large group of mainly short-term prisoners (one-third of the average daily popula-tion, but as many as one-half of all receptions under sentence) who can probably best be described as chronic social casualties, whose pathetic and trivial but persistent offending results in their losing their liberty more because imprison-ment is available than because it is appropriate. All too often, options which would be appropriate are simply not available and so, almost by a process of elimination, imprisonment is the sanction of final resort. The surveys all agree that impris-onment is inappropriate and harmful for these types of offender: the seriousness of their offence does not warrant it; and their clear need for massive social welfare assistance is simply not met within an institutional penal setting.

Moreover all this custody is hopelessly ineffective. A high proportion of offenders enjoy a 'revolving door' relationship with the Prison Department: an unremitting cycle of dis-charge, reoffending and recommittal. About half of all adult prisoners are reconvicted within two years of their leaving prison, with the majority finding themselves back 'inside' within this period. For more youthful offenders the rates of reconviction are sometimes in excess of 80 per cent. And, for the persistent, petty offender – the sort of offender informed opinion would agree least deserves imprisonment – this four-out-of-five failure rate can be regarded as the norm (Home Office, 1978a; Phillpotts and Lancucki, 1979; Home Office, 1981b). In addition, there is a very heavy price to pay for this penal ineffectiveness. It costs over £6,500 a year to keep a man in a local prison, but can cost two or three times as much, depending on the level of security (Shaw, 1980; Home Office, 1981e). These costs are understated, since they exclude the social costs of institutionalization, criminal contamination, and the costs and disruptions caused with regard to family, employment and social ties. To say that imprisonment has a 'deformative' rather than 'reformative' impact on prisoners is not to overstate the case.

In recent years, these matters have received increasing attention and a clear consensus has emerged that a reduction in the prison population must become the major preoccupation of penal policy (Home Office, 1977); this government view was forcibly endorsed by the prestigious Advisory Council on the Penal System (1977, 1978). Similarly, the House of Commons Expenditure Committee (1978) argued that where imprisonment was seen as unavoidable the sentence should be as short as possible, but that where there were no clear-cut reasons for choosing imprisonment, non-custodial sentences ought to be imposed. In response, the government has seen a reduction in demand for prison places as the principal means of bringing relief to an over-burdened and under-resourced prison system (Home Office, 1980a). The basis for this view was one of the recommendations of Mr Justice May who, in his report on the prison system of England and Wales, urged that every effort be made to reduce the prison population (Home Office, 1979b). This view has been even more strongly articulated in two recent reports from the Parliamentary All-Party Penal Affairs Group (1980, 1981).

When the groundswell of informed official opinion is set

alongside the various penal policy initiatives since the 1960s, all intended to keep offenders out of custody altogether or to restrict loss of liberty to a minimum when it was unavoidable (for example parole, suspended and partly suspended prison sentences, community service orders, Day Training Centres, detoxification centres and other shelters for the vagrant alcoholic offender, as well as new experiments in probation supervision), the naïve observer could be forgiven for thinking in terms of the birth of a new Golden Age in community corrections. Prison overcrowding, penal ineffectiveness and high institutional costs all *seem* to point to major, viable, non-custodial alternatives. Imprisonment may now be viewed as a strange relic of a bygone penal era, whilst non-custodial penalties *seem* guaranteed a pre-eminent place in future penal policy (Scull, 1977). Reservations have been expressed, however (Willis, 1981a, 1981c; Pease, 1983), and there are good grounds for distinguishing between penal change and penal progress. It is not sufficient merely to introduce new non-custodial penal options if, in fact, sentencers then choose not to use them. This creates the illusion of change without genuine progress. One of the implications raised in this chapter is that many of the recent innovations turn out to have a substantial rhetorical component and that, in practice, they have done little or nothing to alter the general thrust of government penal policy which is still dominated by an approach based on the widespread use of imprisonment.

Fiscal and political realities

Despite the seemingly impressive collection of official reports about the need to curtail the prison population and the recent introduction of a wide range of apparent alternatives, successive governments have simply failed to deliver significant non-custodial alternatives, and the new age of community corrections remains but a penal pipe-dream. Available research indicates, for example, that less than half of community service orders are made as direct alternatives to custodial dispositions (Pease et al., 1975, 1977; Willis, 1977), and that suspended sentences tend to generate increased rather than lower rates of committals to custody (Bottoms, 1981; Willis, 1981a). Or, to look at matters from a slightly different angle, the decade of the 1970s which witnessed the introduction of all these new non-custodial options was also a period of high and rising rates of imprisonment (Home Office, 1981a). In 1973, some 30,000 offenders were sentenced to immediate imprisonment, but by 1980 the number had increased to 45,000; an increase of 50 per cent. More dramatically, the same period also saw an increase in the proportionate use of custody. In 1973, 11 per cent of all convicted male offenders were deprived of their liberty by the courts, but by 1980 over 14 per cent of them were receiving custodial sentences: an increase from one in nine to one in seven. This trend was most apparent with respect to juvenile male, young adult male and all female offenders where the proportionate use of custody over this period approximately doubled. The evidence of the past ten years is unambiguous: in spite of the introduction of special measures specifically intended to displace from custody, imprisonment is increasingly relied on as a penal sanction of first choice. In consequence, the prison population has risen, is rising and will, in all probability, continue to rise. At present it stands at about 46,000, the highest total ever on record, though by the end of the decade it is estimated it will have reached the 50,000 mark (Home Office, 1979b), which is a clear indication of the Government's commitment to the continued use of prison for offenders for whom it is known to be singularly ineffective and wholly inappropriate. Indeed, the Home Secretary has recently made it clear that the way forward in penal policy is for him to secure the necessary funding for a substantial programme of new prison building (Home Office, 1984), a view echoed by the Chief Inspector of Prisons who also anticipates a population of 50,000 before 1990 (Home Office, 1983). Whatever the heady rhetoric about displacement from custody and community corrections, penal practice is firmly and increasingly underpinned by the sanction of imprisonment.

This burgeoning use of custody presents something of a conundrum: how to explain the almost total frustration of good non-custodial penal intentions by an unrelenting increase in institutional penal practice? The most probable answer, as I have argued elsewhere (Willis, 1981c), is that inertia in prison policy – the seeming inability to bring about a significant shift towards the use of non-custodial sentences even when they are recognized as desirable – is best explained by reference to the political disadvantage and cost-unattractiveness of trying to do anything about the problem. At the publicly visible level of politics, when law and order is a matter of emotional concern, the politician (of any party) who advocates massive reductions in the use of custody would probably commit some form of instant political suicide. Strong advocacy in favour of decarceration, that is keeping offenders out of prison, would only generate Parliamentary brickbats and media disapproval, as well as court electoral disfavour. Although there are no votes in prison, I suspect there are votes to be won by endorsing crime-control strategies which would send ever-increasing numbers there.

This may seem cynical, but the 'war theorists' of criminal justice, those who would happily increase the sum total of penal barbarism, probably have monopolistic control over public sentiment (at least insofar as this is mediated by the popular press) and, in consequence, the ever-sensitive ear of the politicians. Nor is it an adequate reply to point to the various Government and Parliamentary reports referred to earlier which specifically recommend an extension of non-custodial sentences. Closer inspection reveals that these almost exclusively endorse non-custodial penalties for drunks, vagrants, inadequates, mentally-disordered offenders and persons convicted of prostitution-related offences. What they do not do, though, is to point out that in the majority of such cases imprisonment is rarely used and, if used, the sentence is usually short. Nor do they mention that the numbers involved are fairly small. Hence no significant impact would be made in terms of lowering the overall prison population by making these small select groups of offenders not liable to imprisonment. It is all redundant rhetoric. Perhaps that is why it is so frequently bandied about as a solution to the prison problem.

It would be quite a different matter, however, if a serious proposal surfaced to keep out the persistent, petty thieves and burglars who comprise as many as half of all receptions under sentence: something in the order of 25,000 committals each year. This would not be to tinker at the margins of imprisonment, but to engage in a massive restructuring of penal policy. But my guess is that at this point the politicians' nerves would begin to fail: it is one thing to decarcerate drunks, but quite another to foreclose on the option of imprisonment for burglars. In short, expediency would almost certainly dictate that the narrow political interests of not upsetting what the Parliamentarians take to be the vengeful instincts of the general public would prove to be more compelling than meeting the agreed penal policy objectives of promoting alternatives to prison. The former course of action carries no risk and may pay real electoral dividends, whilst the latter is a clear electoral liability.

One example of political timidity was William Whitelaw's refusal to make parole more-or-less automatic for a large number of prisoners. There is no doubt that this would have offered enormous relief to the prison system (Home Office, 1981f), but when he was faced with the implacable opposition of judges and magistrates he readily gave way (*The Sunday Times*, 22 November 1981). This contrasted with his oft-repeated public pronouncements that custody must be avoided whenever possible and that this must be guaranteed, if necessary, by legislation (*The Times*, 14 February 1981; 1 May 1981). Moreover exactly the same thing happened when, despite his acknowledgement that the warehousing of prisoners in the scandalous and 'dungeonlike' conditions of the police cells of the London courts is unacceptable, he publicly refused to use his powers of executive release to ease the difficulties (*The Times*, 19 April 1983). In fact, present penal policy is Janus-faced: the rhetoric of alternatives to custody has been matched by policies tending in the opposite direction.

Nowhere is this more evident than in the policies of Lord Whitelaw's successor at the Home Office, Mr Leon Brittan. In this case, however, it is not a matter of simply doing nothing about the prison problem, but it involves the vigorous pursuit of policies which curry electoral favour by satisfying the punitive instincts of the penal hawks. The Criminal Justice Act 1982, for example, actively promotes custodial sentences: 'toughened up' detention-centre regimes; care orders with a compulsory residential component; and the abolition of Borstal *training* in favour of youth *custody*. Penal policy appears to rely increasingly on the sanction of loss of liberty. In addition, Mr Brittan has authorized the building of 14 new prisons at a capital cost of over £250 million, together with an additional 5,000 prison officers to run these new institutions (Home Office, 1984).

Either way, the crisis deepens. On the one hand political caution guarantees a high and rising prison population because no Home Secretary will take the risk of endorsing a policy which would empty the prisons. It is altogether easier not to do anything about the problem than it is to attempt to resolve it. The political unattractiveness of underwriting real displacement from custody is so great that although any Home Secretary may privately favour such a policy, politically he may well prefer the Opposition spokesman on home affairs to be in office and responsible for it! Alternatively, building more prisons and orchestrating criminal justice policy around the theme of increased penalization may be seen as the way out of the prison crisis. Neither offers a genuine solution.

There are also financial considerations attendant on decarceration. Imprisonment costs on average over £7,000 a year, whilst an equivalent term of probation or a community service order costs under £500 (Shaw, 1980; Home Office, 1981e, 1982a).

There would appear to be a seemingly unanswerable fiscal case for preferring the latter. Unfortunately, this is grossly misleading because it fails to distinguish between the average and marginal costs of custody. The average costs are calculated by dividing the total costs incurred in a given period (usually one year) by the population held over that time, whilst the marginal costs involve only the modest additional expenditure in sending just one more offender to prison. These marginal costs are low, perhaps as little as a few pounds a week, because most of the high fixed costs of imprisonment (the largest being on staff salaries) have already been met. There is only a small additional cost for every new prisoner. Conversely, only marginal savings will be made if penal policy opts to keep small numbers of offenders out of prison.

Strictly speaking, community corrections would prove to be something of a financial embarrassment because they would involve both the high fixed costs of the present prison system *and* the extra expense of providing additional forms of community supervision. In addition, as community support for offenders sought to become more specialized or more comprehensive, these additional costs would soar. Of course, if the switch to non-custodial penalties were to occur on a grand enough scale, sufficient to enable some institutions to be closed down, then real savings could be made. New but modest expenditure on community corrections could be set against huge savings as prisons were closed (and staff made redundant), with the Exchequer happily pocketing the difference. This, though, is most unlikely in the light of the Home Secretary's decision to build 14 new prisons, providing a total of 6,000 additional places (Home Office, 1984). But, unless or until some prisons close down, there is no real prospect of alternatives to custody presenting a compelling financial case.

Promoting displacement from custody

There is no doubt that the combined effect of these factors places real and formidable constraints on the development of non-custodial alternatives to imprisonment, though it is possible to explore some of the available options to assess their feasibility and likely impact. To begin with, what is certainly not required is yet another inventory of possible alternatives to loss of liberty: a sort of catalogue of what might be done or attempted. One such list was put forward by Barnard and Bottoms (1979) who recommended a vast range of options: statutory restrictions on imprisonment, sentencing quotas and sentencing guidelines, improved social inquiry practice, economic incentives, and so on. It is impressive and seems to exhaust all the available options. What is missing, however, is the crucial element indicating which of these strategies would prove both desirable *and* feasible. Stuck in the armchair of penal theory it is a relatively straightforward task to conjure up any number of fanciful displacement plans, but it is quite another matter to suggest practical ones which would work in the real world of penal practice. The simple fact of the matter, as King and Morgan (1980) point out, is that the principle of the minimum use of custody is now generally acknowledged and the range of non-custodial alternatives well known. All that remains is to decide on the appropriate package and then stimulate the political will to implement it. The problem is not one of ignorance about alternatives, but the technical issue of how best to operationalize some of the ideas which have been readily available in recent years. This is a matter of tactics rather than grand strategy, a question of bringing-about-the-possible rather than inventing-the-desirable. The prison problem will not be solved by sending for yet another mail-order penal policy catalogue (good though some of them are); someone, somewhere, has to fill in the order form.

Equally, whatever is going to be done must be done now, or in the immediate future, and must not involve undue delay. This is something King and Morgan (1980) fail to realize when they propose an inter-departmental committee from the Home Office, DHSS and Lord Chancellor's Department to thrash out the details of a penal policy biased towards community corrections. The thought that a range of alternatives could sensibly and quickly be brought to fruition by means of such a committee seems wildly over-optimistic. The most likely scenario is that inter-departmental clashes of interest and Civil Service caution would conspire to secure the slow but certain end of good and bad proposals alike. The committee idea would not promote displacement from custody, it would guarantee inertia. It may be a comforting sop to those who only seek the most marginal and unhurried changes in penal policy, but it affords no prospect of substantial relief to the prison problem. Anything which merely holds out a vague promise of improvement sometime in the indeterminate penal future is irrelevant to the pressing problems of contemporary penal practice. Whatever the solution is, it will have to be firmly and unambiguously located in the penal present, the here-and-now of sentencing practice in the 1980s.

Finally, it is important to stress the simple but often-neglected point that although penal policy often seems immutable, especially in the wake of frustrated attempts at reform, it is in fact nothing more or less than the product of certain legislative and sentencing decisions, which are, at least in principle, reversible. As King and Morgan (1980) correctly observe, the size and composition of the prison population is not a random or predetermined event (like a cold front moving in from the Atlantic), but a simple matter of choice. It is a function of legislative intent as expressed by Parliament, although this is then modified by judicial discretion and executive action, which in turn may be subject to the influence of public opinion. At all of these stages, though with varying degrees of difficulty, decisions which would render someone liable to imprisonment may be subject to change. Unfortunately, in his Inquiry into the United Kingdom prison system and his analysis of possible redirection strategies, Mr Justice May completely overlooks this point (Home Office, 1979b). Although he endorses the familiar rhetoric that the use of imprisonment should be minimized and that redirection is in principle desirable, he concludes that for the foreseeable future Britain will have to support a substantial penal population. He reaches this conclusion because he finds no prospect of genuine alternatives to prison for mentally-disordered or persistent, petty offenders; no chance of widening the use of non-custodial sentences (probation is in irreversible decline, day training is ineffective and costly, hostels are unwelcome and expensive, community service has expanded to its limits, and so on); no room for executive action; and no likelihood of any immediate change in sentencing practice. The fallacy in this line of reasoning lies in is fatalistic acceptance of the sentencing *status quo*, something which a more determined commentator would have sought to challenge rather than accept.

These factors, although they do not suggest anything which would directly lower rates of imprisonment, do point the way towards necessary but not sufficient conditions for effective remedial action. Their negative aspects must be taken into account. The successful implementation of alternatives to custody will have to involve something more than good intentions and grand lists of possible non-custodial sentences; it will need to be of immediate benefit (even if this is modest), rather than hold out the prospect of radical improvement at some time in the future; and it will require exactly the opposite of Mr Justice May's sombre acceptance of the inevitability of an expanding prison population. The next step is to determine the persons or the agencies who might be best placed to engage in this practical, immediate and forceful remedy, although common sense dictates that they will be intimately involved in the sentencing process.

Government, as the initiator of legislation, is certainly able to curb the over-use of custody, but in practice is unwilling to, being far too susceptible to political pressures and fiscal constraints. It is likely to restrict itself to a modest endorsement of the desirability of keeping some offenders out of prison, whilst at the same time investing heavily in new prisons. This way it avoids the costs of providing comprehensive community supervision of offenders, but earns itself political kudos for its tough 'law-and-order' fight against crime. There is no prospect of the Government offering relief.

Nor is there any comfort in assuming, as Lord Whitelaw did (*The Times*, 1 May 1981; *Guardian*, 11 November 1981), that the sentencers in their wisdom could be relied on to use their sentencing powers both wisely and sparingly. Were the climate of opinion amongst the judges and magistrates all that Lord Whitelaw fondly imagined it to be, then there would be no need for legislative or executive action. The prison crisis would simply not exist because sentencers would have shown their willingness to accommodate the prison-reform lobby by changing their sentencing practices so as to progressively restrict the use of custody. The fact that the crisis exists, and is worsening, demonstrates the stupidity of this view. Both legislators and sentencers make poor penal reformers. This means that, discounting legislative initiatives to curb the powers of judges and magistrates, and accepting that the sentencers themselves are most unlikely to put their own house in order, the probation service would appear to stand alone as perhaps the only body involved in the administration of criminal justice in a position to influence sentencing policy. It may not be the most obvious candidate to promote non-custodial sentences, and it may even not relish the prospect. It is, however, the only part of the criminal justice apparatus which is in a position to exercise a moderating influence on the most vindictively penal system in Western Europe (Tulkens, 1979; Fitzmaurice and Pease, 1982). It is arguably the case, therefore, that the probation service is under a double obligation to promote penal reform. This derives both from the unanswerable case that for many offenders (about half of all receptions under sentence) imprisonment is unnecessary and immoral; and it is partly a function of the incapacity of successive Home Secretaries to initiate reform, as well as an intractable judiciary.

The *prima facie* case for believing the probation service to be well placed to secure a degree of displacement from custody derives from the central role it occupies in sentencing, especially in cases involving possible loss of liberty. In these cases an offender will rarely be sentenced without benefit of a social inquiry report. Each year well over 250,000 reports are prepared and presented to the courts (Home Office, 1982a). In the Magistrates' Courts in 1979 the ratio of social inquiry reports to persons proceeded against was about one in five, but for those tried in the Crown Courts the ratio was nine in ten. This suggests that reports are standard practice in the more serious cases: the sorts of case which might well result in deprivation of liberty on conviction. Moreover, the Home Secretary has powers under the Criminal Justice Act 1967 (Section 57) and the Powers of Criminal Courts Act 1973 (Section 45) to make rules to require courts to consider reports in certain cases before passing sentence, although in practice this is done by issuing Home Office Circulars which recommend rather than require reports to be presented (188/1968, 189/1968, 30/1971, 59/1971). The net result of these is that it is normal for the courts to ask for a social inquiry report before imposing a detention centre order, a youth custody sentence, any first custodial sentence, or the imprisonment of any female offender; whenever magistrates refer a case to the Crown Court for sentence; for defendants in the superior courts aged under 31 years, and even for older defendants if they have not received a custodial sentence since their seventeenth birthday; for someone who has recently been in touch with the probation service, or someone subject to a recent medical or psychiatric report; for any woman defendant; and for any person subject to a suspended prison sentence (Home Office, 1978b). Finally, the Powers of Criminal Courts Act 1973 (Sections 19 and 20) requires reports before anyone under the age of 21 years is sent to prison, or when the defendant has not previously been sent to prison.

Certainly all of this is somewhat complicated, but what is both clear and important is that in a very wide range of cases where imprisonment is a likely outcome, the probation service is under an obligation to prepare reports prior to sentence. In fact the trend is towards increasing this requirement. Under the provisions of the Criminal Justice Act 1982, pre-sentence reports are to be asked for in order to determine the most appropriate sentence for all offenders aged under 21 years who are facing possible deprivation of liberty, unless the court thinks it unnecessary in which case it must give its reasons. This makes reports an even more significant variable in the sentencing process. Clearly, the net effect of all these requirements is that offenders who end up in prison should only do so after being sentenced with benefit of a social inquiry report.

In addition, because about 80 per cent of all social inquiry reports contain not just an assessment of the offender and his or her involvement in crime but an explicit recommendation for sentence, and because in over 80 per cent of these cases the recommendation is accepted by the courts, it rather looks as though probation officers and their reports are a major factor in determining eventual sentence (Hine and McWilliams, 1981; Curran, 1983). Indeed, the empirical investigations of social inquiry practice which look beyond the mere level of take-up of recommendations (Mott, 1977; Hine et al., 1978) tend to agree that there is a measurable degree of probation officer influence on sentencing. Of course, the high correspondence between recommendation and sentence could reflect nothing more than the probation officers' ability to second-guess or predict the sentencing intentions of the court (Carlen, 1979), which is then reflected in their recommendations. This may well be true in extreme cases. The gravity of an offence, or its extreme triviality, may be so unambiguous as to make it quite obvious, according to the tariff, that a custodial or nominal penalty, respectively, was a certain outcome. In such instances, the probation officer may tend to second-guess. However, in the range of middle-order cases, although there is undoubtedly some pressure on officers to 'tailor' their reports to the expectations of the bench, it seems implausible to suggest that they never seek to exercise real influence. This would be contrary to government policy which sees pre-sentence reports as a crucial factor in assisting courts in the determination of sentence (Home Office, 1978b): a view firmly reiterated in two recent Home Office circulars (17/1983, 18/1983) which held that reports should contain comprehensive and relevant information, a clearly stated recommendation for sentence and the reasons for it. This being so, social inquiry practice is a crucial element in the process leading to loss of liberty, and one which can have a demonstrable impact on outcome.

The next step is to ask how a reconceptualization of current social inquiry practice can assist in promoting displacement from custody? That some changes are necessary is unarguable. The simple fact of the matter is that the last decade has witnessed a dramatic increase in the use of pre-sentence reports (roughly doubling to about 250,000 each year) and the introduction of a vast range of new non-custodial sentences as alternatives to imprisonment; and yet the proportionate use of custody has also burgeoned. Clearly, present practices will not suffice. Indeed, it is arguably the case that the probation service should be severely taken to task for not already achieving displacement from custody, especially as it so clearly has the means to do so at its disposal. On a more positive note, however, a recent Home Office survey (Fairhead, 1981b) of the way magistrates sentence persistent petty offenders found that in as many as 38 per cent of cases where a prison sentence had been imposed, the magistrates themselves were dissatisfied and would have preferred an alternative non-custodial sentence. Interestingly, fewer than half of the sample had social inquiry reports presented before sentence, and only defendants who had were made the subject of probation orders. This suggests that where reports are used they can offer a realistic route to retention of liberty. Perhaps, then, it is better to look to the future and explore ways of achieving displacement than to dwell on recriminations over missed opportunities.

One idea for avoiding the sanction of imprisonment was put forward by Bottoms and McWilliams (1979), who simply urged that the probation service should cease to be in the business of making any custodial recommendations in their reports. This blanket proscription, they argued, would serve to stimulate imaginative and constructive thought about alternatives. Unfortunately, these fine sentiments contain a logical blunder. Non-custodial recommendations only make sense if they are set against the possibility of custodial ones, just as passing an examination is only credible when it is set against the possibility of failure. It is illegitimate artificially to discard one of two mutually exclusive alternatives (custodial or non-custodial recommendation) and pretend that what is left is a genuine choice. Logic apart, there are additional difficulties at the human level. Would probation officers want, and be willing, to forfeit completely their powers to recommend custody? If they were, what would sentencers make of the new arrangements? How would they interpret a non-custodial recommendation which was only 'lukewarm'? And just what would they infer from the absence of a recommendation altogether? I suspect that they would very rapidly learn to 'see' these as old-style custodial recommendations in disguise. Nothing would have changed.

What the mechanical application of this formula mistakenly tries to do is to circumvent or find an easy way around the problem where no such route exists. If displacement from custody is not to be promoted by ministerial exhortation and will not be brought about by legislation, the probation officer has no option but to meet head-on the intransigence of sentencers which maintains the over-use of custody. There is no alternative other than arguing the non-custodial case for each and every offender he or she would prefer to see not being sent to prison. This task would be far from easy and uncertain in outcome. It cannot be done by somehow out-smarting or out-manœuvring the court and frustrating its sentencing intentions by artificially excluding some possibilities. It can only be done by arguing a case on its merits and convincing the court that a non-custodial sentence is preferable to a term of imprisonment, even where it is known that the court is already contemplating a custodial penalty.

This general argument would have to contain a number of inter-related components. The first requirement would be to expose imprisonment as inappropriate. Its evil and deformative effects, such as institutionalization and criminal contamination, would need to be highlighted, as would its marked lack of beneficial behavioural impact and its huge social and fiscal costs. Second, the court would have to be convinced that a practical alternative would confer some real advantages in respect of the offender. These advantages would have to go further than the mere promise of 'treatment' or 'training' or 'assistance' supposedly on offer in an institutional setting. They could not, however, be so extravagant as to jeopardize credibility. And, third, the proposed alternative would need to satisfy the court's perceived obligation not to impose a noncustodial sentence which would place the public at undue risk. In conjunction, these would constitute the only genuine route to lowering rates of committals to custody. Progress towards community corrections appears to be wholly conditional on the probation service being prepared to 'take on' the sentencers in this way. Nothing else offers any prospect of relief.

It is perfectly clear, however, that each of these arguments could be readily countered. It would be quite possible, for example, for the court to mistakenly but genuinely believe that imprisonment conferred a real formative influence or advantage by way of treatment, training, discipline, basic medical care, shelter, or some such thing, without appreciating its collateral disadvantageous impact. Equally the court may be deeply suspicious of non-custodial programmes which it thinks are insufficiently punitive. It may react negatively to community corrections which seem to pander to the social welfare needs of offenders at the expense of punishment. Finally, it may well be unwilling to run the risk of further criminal depredations by releasing offenders into the community. It may prefer the element of public protection afforded by imprisonment (even if it is of only limited duration), if for no other reason than as a means of securing some temporary relief for victims, police officers and court personnel.

If the probation service accepted this challenge it would guarantee for itself a far more difficult time in court and a much more demanding caseload outside than was formerly the case. In court, probation officers would no longer assume the somewhat restrained role of benign experts who advise the court on matters concerning the socio-pathology of criminality and recommend suitable treatment; rather they would be transformed into the active champions of alternatives to custody, intent on reducing custodial committals. One obvious consequence of this is that the language of social inquiry reports would shift from the pseudo-scientific language of diagnosis (Bean, 1976) to a much higher level of penal policy debate. It may be that officers would become more concerned with matters of culpability and proportionality, the hallmarks of the so-called 'justice' model in corrections (Von Hirsch, 1976). It is certain, however, that the central feature of a reconceptualized social inquiry practice would be to set against the predicted deformative effects of imprisonment a trade-off between the possible benefits to an offender and the risks to society involved in a non-custodial sentence.

Quite apart from the difficulties involved in giving the proper weight to each of these variables in the assessment of what is in the best interests of society and the offender, it is pretty clear that any such strategy would be certain to cause problems concerning probation officers' relations with sentencers. These would arise as officers began to forfeit a measure of credibility with sentencers as they began to argue for alternatives to imprisonment in cases which would have previously seemed obvious candidates for incarceration. A degree of suspicion, and even outright hostility, on the part of sentencers could be expected. Another consequence would be a dramatic fall in the take-up rate of recommendations for sentence as judges and magistrates rejected the new-style advice in some instances. To use a poker-game analogy, sometimes the sentencers would call the officers' non-custodial bluff. These difficulties would conspire to make the preparation and presentation of reports a much more onerous task.

Outside courts, too, professional life would be very different. To the extent that probation officers were successful in displacing offenders from custody, they would now be using community-based sentences for the more marginal and less tractable types of offender: the sort who would formerly have been sent down. Irrespective of the type of criminal supervision (existing alternative or new measure, probation-based or not), 'caseloads' would almost certainly increase and, more significant, would become that much more difficult to manage. At present criminal supervision in the community is almost exclusively reserved for the relatively young, not-too-serious offender (Home Office, 1982a), but under the revised scheme of things all this would change. The supervision of offenders in the community would move 'up-market' and become that much more demanding.

In addition, because of this shift in the profile of offenders, the prospect of breakdown and reconviction would be substantially increased, especially in the early days when the probation service was still adjusting to the new demands and experimenting with innovatory styles of supervision. It could be that the courts would lose patience with the new measures even before initial teething troubles had been ironed out. Moreover, sooner or later, community correctional programmes would have to be subject to scrutiny and assessment, and the probation service would have to prove that they 'worked', to the satisfaction of themselves, the sentencers and the general public. In particular, they would need to spend some considerable amount of time reassuring the sentencers, who may well see their primary obligation as being to society and not the offender, that these community alternatives conferred real benefits on offenders without placing the public at undue risk. Probation officers would certainly have to demonstrate measurable effects in both crime control (for the benefit of society) and social welfare assistance or correction (for the benefit of the offender), and also convince sentencers that the prospect of further criminality and breakdown in some cases was an acceptable price to pay for displacement from custody, and the avoidance of all the evil and deformative effects associated with loss of liberty. This suggests that any reconceptualization of social inquiry practice is but a prelude to a fundamental re-examination of the purpose and nature of criminal supervision in the community. It is, however, a necessary beginning. Without it, displacement from custody cannot take place.

Conclusion

Although there is general acceptance of the desirability of displacement from custody, there is no certainty about its feasibility. Indeed, sentencing data from the last decade suggest ever-increasing recourse to loss of liberty (Home Office, 1981a). Political timidity on the part of governments, which fear an electoral backlash should they be seen to endorse removing people from prison, together with their unwillingness to bear the additional costs of new non-custodial options, means that inertia prevails in penal policy. As a consequence, the prison population is likely to increase. This is the sombre outlook, although there is just one prospect of remedy. If any progress is to be made, the probation service will have to tackle the intransigence of sentencers head-on. Social inquiry practice would need to be re-jigged so that imprisonment became articulated as inappropriate and harmful, whilst non-custodial alternatives would need to be marketed as worthwhile in themselves, without posing any undue threat to society. By any yardstick, this is a formidable task. It would be unrealistic, therefore, to conjure up a romantic image of a new Golden Age in corrections, one which will witness the state-sponsored abolition of custodial penalties. It is possible, though, by means of the strategies outlined above, to take steps to guarantee that institutional methods of social control are used progressively less frequently.

3

The Close Support Unit: An Intermediate Treatment Provision for those at Risk of Removal from the Community

Peter Murray

The place of the CSU[1] in the 'continuum of care'

It has long been recognized that IT is not a singular concept or a description of a particular form of provision, but refers to a range of provisions aimed at juveniles who are either known offenders or thought to be at risk of offending (Paley and Thorpe, 1974). The range covers all provisions for the care of youth between 'Basic and Universal Provisions: schools, community facilities, youth clubs' and 'Residential Care: community schools and homes, detention centres and Borstals (86). Paley and Thorpe go on to argue that the continuum of care afforded by IT is open, which: 'suggests that intermediate treatment, far from being one of three possibilities [supervision, intermediate treatment and residential care], absorbs nearly all ... possibilities' (87).

Other early attempts to explain IT in terms of a 'continuum of care' demonstrate its conceptual openness. For example, Tutt (1976) referred to its synthesizing properties in welding together various already existing approaches to care and delinquency management of children and young people. These ranged from preventative measures, based on providing alternative activities to illegal ones and those aimed at promoting new opportunities and skills. On the other hand, community-based programmes intended to provide alternatives to custody featured in early theorizing about IT. Since the early 1980s the general trend in IT provision has been towards such alternative to custody programmes, although the period has also witnessed a dramatic increase in the use of custody for young offenders (Willis, chapter 2).

Reference to the concept of a 'continuum of care' has its advantages and disadvantages. The main disadvantage is that issues of care become entangled with issues of delinquency with the result that the concept of IT is vague, meaning 'all things to all men' (Bottoms and Sheffield, 1980). Second, the use of the word continuum implies an unbroken succession of stages, each one slightly higher up the scale of provision than the last. However, the range of provisions available is insufficient to conclude that an unbroken continuum of increasing intensity of supervision and intervention actually exists. There is, moreover, a qualitative distinction to be made between provisions made in the community and those based in institutional settings, even though IT activities occur in both settings.

The advantage of seeing IT in broad terms as a 'continuum of care' is that the provisions made can be diverse, and activities can involve a range of juveniles, from those at risk of offending to those at risk of being removed from the community. This means also that 'alternative to custody' type projects can be based on activities offering 'new opportunities' type approaches to dealing with delinquent behaviour. The CSU is a project of this kind.

'Alternatives to custody' and 'new opportunities' projects lie at opposite ends of IT provisions, as originally proposed by Paley and Thorpe in 1974. Paley and Thorpe (1974, 91) see differences in terms of the 'increasing intensity of supervision, intervention and treatment', as one approaches provisions associated with alternatives to custody. Differences may also be seen in terms of relative degrees of 'care' and 'control'. At the 'new opportunities' end the major emphasis is on care, with control being only a minor part. Progression to the 'alternatives to custody' end involves an increase in the degree of control, whilst the amount of care, it is argued, remains constant.

The CSU, then, is an IT provision which, in terms of the above analysis, places equal emphasis on care and control. It is the balancing of control with care or support which enables control to be seen in a positive light. However, Fullwood (1976, 38) has implied that control and support may be confused, since they: 'overlap and influence each other and in the final analysis one has a series of complex interrelated systems and considerable difficulty in actually identifying which activities are to be defined as control and which as support'.

The author then goes on to make a statement that underlies the central theme of the CSU and any similar project:

Control can be imposed from without by others or from within by the individual concerned, and some would say the latter is the only true and helpful kind of control. The probation officer can be seen as an imposer of outside control, he can also be seen as encouraging and enabling the individual to develop his own control. (38)

The structure of the CSU and achieving the balance between care and control

The CSU is one branch of the Medway Centre, the others being the Probation Control Unit, the Day Training Centre, and the Medway Community Service Centre. The Medway Centre as a whole is managed by a Senior Probation Officer, who is the line manager of the Probation Officer responsible for the CSU. The other staff directly involved in the CSU are two supervisors and the 'unit mother'. The latter four were all interviewed for the purposes of this research over a one-week period, each interview lasting on average 50 minutes.

It appears that there is great emphasis in the CSU placed upon the concept of the family, with all of its implications for

care and control. One of the supervisors sees himself in the
elder brother role, the role of the other being more as a father
figure. The role of the unit mother is self-explanatory. The
Probation Officer in charge of the unit also takes on the role of
father figure, though he is more the maker of rules: a head of
the household type figure.

Within these roles the unit staff aim to dispense both care
and control, as would happen in any family situation, and the
CSU emphasizes both these functions of their jobs. The CSU
'manual' states that the unit staff: 'will provide (at the end of
the school or working day) the trainees with a good meal in
supportive environment, which will be tuned to cope with
both the physical and emotional needs of what will amount to
a large family of adolescent children' (Sussex, 1978, 28). In the
same document the following statement is made:

The atmosphere aimed for, in the unit, should be such that trainees
will be happy to attend thus lessening their awareness of supervision
at any given time. Inevitably, adolescents will test the system and it
is important that staff adopt a consistent attitude at all times. In the
main, control will be maintained by a limit setting process and
trainees who exceed the limit will be disciplined through withdrawal
of privileges and the imposition of fatigues. (Sussex, 1978, 34)

The nature of the programme at the unit is intended to
maintain a balance between care and control. The programme
is a mixture of supervised work, both academic and physical,
and recreational activities. It is assumed that the staff establish
their control function within the work situation (where it is
argued it is seen as legitimate by the clients), and that control
can then be applied, if necessary, to the more 'caring'
environment of the recreational situation (where in isolation
control may appear illegitimate to the clients). This means that
the programme can cover a wide range of activities available in
IT. Indeed the programme provided by the CSU includes all
categories listed in Paley and Thorpe (1974, 88–9).

Advantages and disadvantages as seen by the staff

The CSU is seen by staff to have advantages over both the custodial setting and the traditional field setting. The Medway Centre Annual Report states that:

The unit programme is designed to ensure that trainees gain maximum benefit from close supervision without the disadvantages associated with institutional treatment. Trainees remain at home and as far as possible within their normal environment, thus ensuring that any treatment is in the context of, and not in isolation from, the cause of delinquency. (1981, 3)

These sentiments are reflected in the advantages the staff associate with the CSU over a custodial setting. One, for example, saw the unit as an 'opportunity to present authority in a positive light to clients'. Another saw advantage in the fact that clients remain in the community: 'they don't get out of the habit of being outside.'

The staff also felt that the CSU setting has advantages over traditional supervision mainly in terms of the increased intensity of supervision which is possible. As one member of staff commented, this means: 'the minor problems can be picked up at an earlier stage ... and therefore are prevented from becoming major problems.' Further, the fact that a client can be sure he will always see a face he knows at the unit between 9 a.m. and 9 p.m. is, in the opinion of staff, of great comfort to him. The staff also welcome the opportunity of working with clients all the time, whether at the unit or on activities. This situation was contrasted with traditional supervision, with its reliance on short and formal periods of contact.

One member of staff felt that there were no disadvantages to working with clients in the CSU setting. The others, however, did see disadvantages both in regard to clients building up a dependency on the unit, and because of the rigidity of the programme and rules. To expand on the first disadvantage, one member of staff felt that there was a possibility of the unit becoming 'a glorified youth club', especially if 'ex-clients keep coming back, and treating it as an exclusive club'. He felt, moreover, that: 'there is a danger of them becoming totally dependent on the unit and after 90 days (they) will be back to square one.' In order to avoid this happening, great emphasis is placed on encouraging clients to develop their own re-creational activities outside the unit.

Working within a rigid programme and set of rules can have disadvantages for clients, according to one member of staff. For example, the rigidity of the programme can mean that:

Client contact and problems are relegated to convenient times for both parties ... A client may come in, in the morning, with problems relating to his home situation and report to the Day Training Centre manager. However, if the programme says he should go job hunting he will be told to go there, and therefore cannot see the probation officer until later. If the probation officer is on court duty, it could be the next day before he sees the client.

This also reflects the problem of divided responsibilities in that the Day Training Centre's job is to make sure the clients attend the workshop and job-hunting sessions, whilst it is the probation officer's job to sort out the client's problems.

The rules of the unit are outlined in the CSU policy document and some staff said that they feel they 'have no autonomy over them'. They can interpret them, but if they are then 're-interpreted by the senior this can lead to chaos'. It would appear, then, that the rigid code of rules, seen by management as necessary for the running of a unit such as the CSU, may stifle the progress and autonomy of the officers working with the clients. Further, the need for a clear division of responsibilities coupled with strict adherence to a set programme means clients' problems are dealt with at organiza-tionally convenient times rather than when they arise.

The clients' views

It is important to consider the place of the CSU within the range of IT provisions, together with its aims and the views of its staff about working in such an environment, in relation to clients' views. This section will consider how clients perceive the unit, its regime, its functions and its effects on them. The material used is based on interviews with 10 clients on the unit probation officer's caseload in September 1982. Five clients were at that time attending the unit plus five who had left and were under the supervision of an outside probation officer; that is, they still had part of their supervision orders to run. Although the length of the interviews varied, they lasted on average 30 minutes, and were conducted over a period of about two weeks.

All the clients interviewed felt they would have gone to detention centre or Borstal had they not been placed on supervision with the CSU condition. All but one said they had been told, either in court or by their social worker, that they would otherwise have received a custodial sentence; the other said he felt in his own mind he would have. Only half of those interviewed, however, could say why they had been given a supervision order rather than a custodial sentence. First offenders felt that the objective was to 'get it out of [them] before they got worse'; more experienced offenders felt it was to 'give [them] a last chance to start again'.

Although one client interviewed felt the best thing about the CSU was 'going home, because I can't stand the place', others were more positive in their attitudes. Some felt the best aspect was the activities, both recreational – 'the bowling, football and pool', 'being taken out and not having to pay' – and educational – 'doing homework here is good, we have tutors, it's more personal than at school'. Others were perhaps a little more philosophical, and considered their continued freedom as the best thing about the CSU. For one, 'still having my

freedom' was what mattered most; for another it was the way
the unit compared with custody: 'we're not locked up all the time
here.' Other clients welcomed the effort that was being made
to keep them out of trouble; for these the care and support of
staff was seen as the best feature of the unit. One client
commented that: 'keeping out of trouble was the best thing
about the CSU'; another that: 'here you are taught a lesson,
the curfew[2] keeps you off the streets so you can't get into
trouble.' For these clients, the supervisors were seen as: 'a
good laugh', who worked 'just like a family who ... keep you
out of trouble'.

Perhaps inevitably 'chores' were looked upon as being the
worst thing about the CSU; that is, the fact that there is a set
rota for doing the washing-up and tidying the dining room
after meals. One (male) client felt that: 'it is women's work',
although the others gave no particular reason why they
disliked chores. One client mentioned the workshop as the
worst aspect of the unit.

The complexity of client responses to questions about the
best and worst aspects of the unit indicates the impossibility of
designing a programme which accommodates everybody's
likes. Whereas one of the respondents quoted above felt that
doing homework at the unit was the best thing about it,
another commented: 'having to do homework is the worst
thing, when I first came here I'd left school but I still had to do
homework.' Whilst some clients saw positive aspects to the
curfew, in terms of helping to keep them out of trouble, others
saw it as the worst feature of the unit. There were other
opinions falling between these extremes, such as: 'the curfew
is the worst thing because of the time it's at, if it was later it
would be OK.' The purpose of the curfew was distinguished
from custody by clients, however.

With regard to custody, no client could name any aspect of a
custodial institution which they could say was 'best', or even
one that was 'least worst'. Their responses reflected their
previous custodial experience, inasmuch as those with such
experience gave more rational, less impressionistic, responses.

Some clients felt that: 'the discipline isn't a bad thing'; and one said that: 'providing I got on with other people it wouldn't bother me.' In general, clients said that the worst aspect about custody was the 'loss of freedom', and some added: 'being locked up 24 hours a day'. Others felt that besides loss of freedom there was also the threat of physical violence from 'other lads bigger than me'. Finally, some of the non-experienced respondents said they had 'never thought about it', and therefore couldn't say what the worst aspects would be.

As for the rules of the unit, all bar two respondents gave 'obeying the curfew' as one of the most important rules. The importance of obeying the rules was generally recognized. 'If you're told to do something, you do it', and, 'obeying orders straight away', were typical replies. For some clients, however, there appeared to be confusion between the aims of the unit and its rules. For example, one felt the most important rules were: 'to get a job, to try to stay out of trouble and to learn to depend on yourself'; another that: 'having good manners and cleanliness' were the most important rules. Other 'rules' mentioned were 'not swearing', 'going to work or school', 'coming in on time' and 'doing your chores'.

The clients, in general, had a good knowledge of the rules of the unit, and they all said they had been told to learn them. One commented that the probation officer 'tells us everything we must do and what we can't do and explains what they mean'. Some clients have vague notions that it is the Senior Probation Officer who makes the rules, although others said they did not know who makes the rules. All of those talked to, however, identified the supervisors as the ones who made sure they kept the rules. In general, it appears to be unimportant to the clients precisely who makes the rules or why; importance is attached to learning them, knowing that the supervisors will enforce them and knowing what will happen if they are broken.

The system of punishments was felt to be fair by all but two of the clients, and neither of these actually said it was unfair.

One said he did not know if it was fair, and another
commented: 'it doesn't bother me much, there isn't much I
can do about it anyway.' The system of punishments is
perceived by clients to depend on the nature of misdemeanours and on the seriousness of infractions. Minor infringements would warrant a warning the first time and extra
chores the next time. For more serious infringements such as
breaking the curfew, they felt they would be taken back to
court. Many of those interviewed mentioned the fact they
would be 'given a chance for the first time', but they also
'knew' they would be 'sent to Borstal' for repeated infringements.

For all but one of the clients interviewed, the question of
what happens if they broke the rules was hypothetical as they
had not actually broken rules or been caught doing so. Hence
the question of the system being fair was not answered on the
basis of direct experience. What the clients seemed to be
saying was that it was fair that if somebody broke the rules he
should be punished. Whether they would have the same
attitude to their own misdemeanours and subsequent punishment is not known. However, the one client who had infring-
ed the rules (he had spat out of a window) felt that: 'being
given chores to do was a fair punishment'. Another client
commented upon the positive element of punishments: 'they
are just right,' he said, 'it teaches you a lesson just when you
need it at the right time'. Although all of those interviewed
had an idea of what would happen to them if they broke the
rules, one gained the impression that it was based on hearsay
and on what had been passed on by others rather than on
anything they had been told by staff.

Clients' views about the wider aspects of staff roles in the
unit formed an important area of discussion during the
interviews. Only one client saw the Probation Officer's job as
anything to do with him personally; he felt the officer's job
was to: 'just sort of keep an eye on you and see how you're
getting on'. The others all saw the Probation Officer as some
sort of overall controller/manager, though one felt he 'acts as a

go-between, between the supervisors and the senior probation officer'. One client outlined the officer's job as: 'making sure the supervisors knew what was going on and what had to happen'. Another highlighted the Probation Officer's 'arbiter' role: 'if you're mad with the supervisors you see him, he makes sure you're behaving yourself.'

The clients did not readily identify the unit Probation Officer as their counsellor/supervisor. They were asked more specifically, however, what the Probation Officer's job meant to them personally. The response to this question was mixed: about half felt that the Probation Officer had no job with them personally, either because: 'I see the supervisor if I've got problems', or, 'I've got my probation officer outside.' This latter comment was made because, at the time the interviews were conducted, it was policy for unit clients to return to their outside probation officers after the 90 days' programme within the unit had been completed. The outside probation officer also tended to be very involved during the 90-day period, perhaps to the exclusion in the eyes of the client of the unit Probation Officer. Of the others, some saw the unit Probation Officer's job in relation to them as a counsellor: 'arranging things, making sure you're OK', or, 'I go to him for a friendly chat', or, 'I know I can talk to him about my problems.' The remaining group saw his relationship to them in less personal terms: 'I see him every week to see how I'm getting on', or [if] I've got any problems' were typical comments from this group.

The majority of clients interviewed did not know precisely what the unit Probation Officer was expected to do. Comments made, such as: 'I didn't bother to find out, I prefer the supervisors better than the probation officer', suggest that the Probation Officer's job does not concern the majority of clients as long as they do not meet him in his disciplinary capacity. Those who felt the unit Probation Officer was doing the job they expected him to do were those who saw his job in less personal terms, i.e. the person they went to see from time to time to make sure they were getting on all right. One person felt that the Probation Officer was not doing the job he expected, explaining: 'I thought he was supposed to be in charge but then I found out it was the senior who was really.'

Perhaps the most important opinion of the clients is what they feel the CSU can do for them. Only two of those interviewed made negative comments; one felt it was 'a complete waste of time, only you can change yourself'. What the others emphasized was the help and care available at the CSU, contrasting this with the lack of these things at Borstal or detention centre. One said that: 'here they try to help you get a job, but in Borstal the people just don't care.' Others said: 'I feel I came to the CSU for rehabilitation not punishment'; 'all you do in Borstal is plan to re-offend, when you get out of the CSU you don't'; 'you can relax in the CSU, but you can't in DC, you can't talk to people either.' Following the fact that many cited the recreational facilities as the best thing about the unit, it is not surprising that the CSU was compared so favourably to Borstals or detention centres. The forming of positive relationships with staff was also an area of favourable comparison, as clients felt this could never happen in Borstals or detention centres.

Many clients emphasized the help they were receiving in the CSU as being related to their keeping out of trouble. This was seen as a real achievement since for most of their time they were living outside the unit, and hence the opportunities to offend were still available, unlike the situation in custodial institutions.

If they had a chance to change the CSU, over half the clients interviewed would do nothing. They felt that what the CSU does 'is adequate', 'pretty fair as it is', 'is alright as it is, they do it all for you'. Most would not want to change any rules, with the possible exception of making the curfew time later. The absence of rules to one client: 'would mean chaos, the supervisors wouldn't be able to control'. One client did not even want the curfew to be changed, because: 'if it wasn't for that I know I'd be out every night.'

Only one client wanted changes amounting to closing the unit down, saying: 'there shouldn't be a Close Support Unit. If it wasn't for the fact I have to see the probation officer every week, I wouldn't come.' Inevitably, there were some comments about doing away with all the chores and abolishing the curfew, but most changes mentioned were minor in character.

Conclusion

In this paper it has been argued that the CSU constitutes a valid approach to dealing with serious young offenders; that is, those who would have stood a very good chance of receiving a custodial sentence if the unit were not available. More specifically it is suggested that IT schemes operating as alternatives to custody can successfully balance care and control, and provide clients with help which they seem to appreciate. Reaching a balance between care and control is problematic, both from the point of view of social work practice and justice. Moreover, the clients for whom the CSU is intended are fairly sophisticated and maintaining such a balance presents formidable practical problems: too much control would make people feel they were in an institution, and with too little, the structured nature of the setting would begin to break down.

It is the control aspect which sets the CSU, and other intensive alternatives to custody provisions, apart from other forms of IT. The emphasis on control has resulted in the unit becoming subject to extensive criticism within the probation service. Walker and Beaumont (1981) have maintained that this also renders the work undertaken in the unit unprofessional, the wider implications of which: 'could so change the probation role that negatives predominate and opportunities for useful work ... become so limited that the job becomes unacceptable' (162). The writers go on to castigate the CSU, seeing it as an exemplar of projects, orders or licences involving 'extreme measures of control over clients', which serve to undermine the traditions, autonomy and prime purposes of probation work.

Judging from the client responses in this paper, the control aspect of the CSU does not appear to have an overbearing profile. Naturally they see control in a different light from outside commentators, but also seem to accept the objective of the unit to balance control with care and welfare considerations, and, in my view, clients did not have positive views about control merely because of fears as to the effects of non-compliance regarding the unit's rules.

The main problem in trying to assess clients' views about alternatives to custody is that compared to custody anything is preferable. This case is no exception. Clients tended to compare the CSU with the negative qualities of custody, particularly the total loss of liberty involved with Borstals and detention centres. However, certain positive things were said or implied about the CSU, which show that clients do perceive the unit as a worthwhile alternative to custody because, unlike custody, tangible forms of help are offered in the CSU.

Despite the high visibility of rules in the CSU, the system of rules and punishment was felt to be at least fair, and in one case absolutely right. Again and again the clients emphasized the help they were being given to stay out of trouble, and it would seem they both appreciated this help and saw it as related to the control inherent to the unit.

Although no client actually said so in the course of this research, it may be suggested that many were learning self-control, as distinct from externally imposed control, while attending the unit. This is not to deny the importance of such external controls or the relatively powerless position clients were in, in relation to staff. Thus the references made to the concept of the family by clients may have been because of an acceptance of the staff's ideology, or may indicate correspondence between staff and client views. This research does not provide definitive answers to such problems. However, it does demonstrate that clients are able to distinguish the rules of the unit from the individuals enforcing them. Despite these rules and the structured nature of the setting, some clients could get sufficiently close to some members of staff to enable care and support to be both offered and received. It is interesting that the set-up of the CSU does not allow the Probation Officer to adopt this role: in the view of the clients, he must stand back, be aloof, and make judgements. The Probation Officer's position seems problematic in that he is the only staff member to have a clear-cut controlling role.

To conclude, what was described by subjects in the course of interviews may not have been a controlling environment but rather a highly structured one, relying on a balance between care and control such as to enable clients to learn and exercise self-control. This research provides some evidence that clients learn to conform to rules and to the expectations of others, to build up trust in their relations to others, and to establish for themselves the importance of keeping out of trouble. Whether such benefits are sustained over time, and include the period after leaving the CSU, cannot be answered until more detailed and longitudinal research is undertaken. Albeit tentatively, the unit can be seen as a relevant example of an alternative to custody programme operating within a structured setting: and one which avoids the damaging effects of imprisonment upon subjects. Provision of such alternatives is necessary if social work with young people who commit serious offences is to continue. Furthermore, a high degree of control and direction over the lives of serious young offenders is needed, since otherwise alternatives would lack credibility with both sentencers and the public at large.

NOTES

1   The CSU programme, developed jointly by the Kent Probation Service and Social Services Department in 1978, is based on the provisions of the 1969 Children and Young Persons Act as amended by the 1977 Criminal Law Act, specifically Section 12 (subsection 1–3). The programme offered the provision of supervision 12 hours

per day for 5 days per week from 9.00 a.m. to 9.00 p.m. (later changed to 8.00 p.m.) and involvement in a task of value to the community from 9.00 a.m. to 4.00 p.m. on Saturdays. The programme lasted for a total of 90 days, after which the client continued on 'normal' supervision for the remainder of his order.

At the time of writing, the CSU is being run down and is due to close in the spring of 1984. The reasons for this are complex, but have much to do with first, the large drop in the number of juveniles appearing before Medway Court and second, a desire by Kent Social Services Department to set up their own scheme aimed at the same target group. The point is that the CSU has not had to close due to the failure of the principles on which it was developed, but due to a lack of suitable clients and the consequent increase in cost.

2   Curfew hours are between 10.00 p.m. and 6.00 a.m. the next morning; to be out of the house between those times is an infringement of the rules.

4

The Driver Retraining Scheme: Towards Managing Autocrime

Peter Harraway

Introduction

This paper describes an approach to dealing with offenders convicted of taking and driving away (TDA) and its related offences: that is, allowing to be carried, attempted TDA, driving without insurance, licence, etc. The Driver Retraining Scheme uses a standard probation order (i.e. without special conditions) as its legal framework, and is therefore applicable to defendants aged 17 and above, convicted in the adult Magistrates' Courts and Crown Courts. The type of offender the programme is aimed at is familiar to probation officers as the 'TDA merchant' or 'car freak', whose criminal activities usually, if not exclusively, centre on cars. These offenders are generally under 21 years of age and almost always male. The vast majority do not possess provisional driving licences and have had little formal driving tuition. Despite this, they can usually handle cars competently and have gained experience through illegal driving. The majority have a keen interest in cars and driving which, in itself, is quite legitimate. It is the way

I would like to thank John Abbott, Amanda Brown, Chris Hignett, Anna Keegan, Sarah Mortimer and Iolanda Wilson, probation colleagues at the Demonstration Unit, for their help in operating the Driver Retraining Scheme and contributing to this paper; also to acknowledge the contribution of Jim O'Reilly (Senior Probation Officer), Martyn Elliott and Mike Nicolson (Probation Officers) in ILPS for their help in the early development of the scheme.

in which they pursue this interest that brings them into conflict with the law. The TDA offender can be seen as someone who uses illegitimate means to pursue legitimate ends. The problem of managing such offenders in the community, therefore, becomes one of diverting their interest into legitimate channels which will achieve the ends they want.

The origins and development of the Driver Retraining Scheme lie in the response of the Inner London Probation Service (ILPS) to the problems which TDA offenders pose for sentencers, probation officers, and for the communities in which offenders live and commit their offences. The Driver Retraining Scheme forms a part of the task of the Demonstration Unit in ILPS. The Unit is composed of a team of six officers and was set up in the North-East Division of ILPS in July 1981. It draws clients from the three Magistrates' Courts in the boroughs of Hackney, Islington and Tower Hamlets; that is, Old Street, Highbury Corner and Thames Magistrates' Courts. Prior to the start of the Unit, two preliminary driver retraining groups had been run in 1980–1, with results which encouraged a wider trial of the idea. This paper will describe the scheme as it has operated between October 1981 and December 1983. During this period the status of the scheme has been developmental, and the objective has been to test its effectiveness.

Referral to the scheme occurs when a court remands a defendant convicted of TDA (or a similar offence) for a social inquiry report prior to sentencing. During the 20 months that the scheme took referrals, 132 offenders have been referred, resulting in 80 offenders being placed on probation after the courts have considered social inquiry report recommendations. It should be noted that until June 1982 the scheme was available only at the Old Street Court, but has since been extended to the other local courts referred to above, with a corresponding increase in referrals. Referrals to the experimental scheme ceased in July 1983, when the scheme was transferred to operate from normal field offices in the three boroughs. Referrals to field offices commenced in October

1983 and are continuing with the scheme being operated in the field as a normal part of probation activities.

Autocrime and the origins of the Driver Retraining Scheme

Offenders convicted of TDA comprise a substantial proportion of defendants appearing before the Old Street, Highbury Corner and Thames Magistrates' Courts; that is approximately 10 per cent of all sentenced defendants, excluding those convicted solely of drunkenness offences. Internal surveys carried out by the Inner London Probation and After-care Service in 1980, 1981 and 1982 indicate that there is little variation in the proportion of defendants appearing for this particular offence. Previously these defendants were more likely to receive heavier sentences than those committing other common offences, with the exception of burglary. Typically these sentences included: detention centre, short prison sentences, committal to Crown Court for sentence (usually resulting in a Borstal sentence) and community service. It is expected that with the new youth custody sentences, introduced by the Criminal Justice Act 1982, the tendency for TDA offenders to receive custodial sentences will increase. The afore mentioned surveys indicated that, except amongst first offenders, fines and discharges were not usual and disqualification from driving was often imposed in addition to the sentence. In the period before the introduction of the Driver Retraining Scheme, probation was used less often than with other types of offence, and this was mainly because probation officers infrequently made probation recommendations in their reports on TDA offenders.

The 1980 Inner London Probation and After-care Service (ILPAS) Survey of Social Enquiry Reports and subsequent survey work in 1981 show that probation was recommended in less than 20 per cent of reports written on TDA offenders. This compared with a figure of 27 per cent of probation recommendations on offenders convicted of theft, burglary, assault, sexual offences, drugs, etc. This finding suggests that probation officers tended previously to avoid working with TDA offenders. However, TDA offenders did come under supervision at a later stage, when released on licence from detention centres and Borstals, so probation officers' tendency to avoid working with TDA offenders on probation may have resulted in propelling such offenders into custody.

The reasons for the relatively low level of probation recommendations made are complex, but there is no reason to suppose that sentencers were unwilling to accept a probation recommendation on TDA offenders. The courts followed *all* probation recommendations made in the survey periods in 1980 and 1981 on TDA offenders, i.e. in the period before the scheme was set up. This figure compares well with the average concordance rate between recommendation and sentence of around 68 per cent (1980 ILPAS Survey of Social Enquiry Reports). It would seem that part of the explanation was that many probation officers felt that they had little to offer the repeating TDA offender, who often does not present the kind of social, interpersonal and emotional problems with which probation officers feel they can help. In terms of their social and family backgrounds, TDA offenders do not seem to be noticeably or consistently different from their non-delinquent peers living in the same area. They generally live at home with their families, are unemployed or working in unskilled jobs, and mostly 'failed' at school. However, very few own vehicles, and vehicles are rarely owned by other members of their families. Possibly the factor of vehicle ownership and experience differentiates autocrime offenders from non-offenders.

Before the scheme was set up more than one of the local stipendiary magistrates commented to the author on the difficulties in sentencing TDA offenders. Their feeling was that, except for first offenders, they had little option but to impose custodial sentences, albeit sometimes suspended (it is interesting to note that since the 1982 Criminal Justice Act, the power to suspend sentences on offenders under 21 years of age has been removed). They appreciated the negative effects of disqualification from driving for adolescents who want to drive, since this would prevent them from taking any steps to legitimize their interest for the duration of the driving ban. In the absence of alternatives to custodial sentences for more serious offenders, magistrates considered that they had little alternative but to move up quickly from fines and disqualifications to custodial sentences. None of the disposals that were used helped the young person to legitimize his or her driving, and even fines worked against this since paying a fine often hinders a defendant from paying for licences, driving tests and driving lessons. Disqualification from driving, even for a short period of six or twelve months, can actively cause further offending if the young person ignores the ban and is arrested for driving whilst disqualified.

The problem of autocrime can be seen as a result of the frequency with which it occurs, the generally low level of appropriate intervention by probation officers, and the fact that traditional sentencing practices fail to deter subsequent offending and, in some cases, actively cause further offending. Failure to solve the problem is serious, since TDA offenders are a severe nuisance to the people whose cars are taken and, because they drive uninsured, they pose a substantial risk to other road users.

Content and objectives of the Driver Retraining Scheme

The Driver Retraining Scheme was explicitly designed to tackle the problems posed by the TDA offender. Its overall aim is to hold TDA offenders in the community, through helping them to change from illegitimate to legitimate driving behaviour, and to redirect their interest in driving and vehicles towards legality. Through this process the probation service's involvement with TDA offenders is substantially increased, and the court is offered a sentencing alternative which can avoid the negative effects of other types of sentence, and custodial sentences in particular.

With a small number of exceptions, the Driver Retraining Scheme restricts referrals to those defendants who have two or more previous convictions, not necessarily for TDA, in addition to a most recent conviction for TDA. This was done for several reasons, not least to bring the scheme in line with other work which is undertaken at the Demonstration Unit. In terms of extending the use of probation, staff wanted to exclude, as far as possible, those defendants most likely to receive discharges and fines at the Magistrates' Courts. From the survey work already referred to, first offenders are very unlikely to receive heavier sentences than a fine, and so were excluded to avoid 'net widening'. The intended extension of the use of probation was to be in the area previously occupied by detention centres, prisons (including suspended sentences), committals to higher courts with a recommendation for Borstal training, and community service.

At the courts where the Driver Retraining Scheme is in operation, sentencing trends revealed by a survey work undertaken in 1982 demonstrate a substantial increase in the use of probation for TDA offenders. However, there has been a smaller, but still appreciable, drop in the use of custodial sentences – whether suspended or not – and also community service. This would suggest that the scheme may not have been entirely successful in avoiding drawing into the 'net' of provision offenders who would otherwise have received low-tariff sentences.

The scheme aims to be as non-selective as possible. All defendants remanded for social inquiry reports are referred to the scheme if they meet the minimal criteria of conviction of an offence of TDA and possession of two or more previous convictions. A few defendants are not referred because they live outside the London boroughs of Hackney, Islington and Tower Hamlets and must be supervised in their home area. If defendants are already under statutory supervision with colleagues they are not usually referred, but sometimes a transfer of the case is arranged. A small number of first offenders were, however, accepted on the scheme from Old Street Magistrates' Court for historical reasons.

Referrals are interviewed by the two probation officers leading each Driver Retraining course, and a social inquiry report is then prepared and presented to the court at the time of sentence. In 73 per cent of referrals a probation order is recommended, and the courts have followed these recommendations for 83 per cent of cases. Consequently 61 per cent of all referrals have resulted in a probation order being made at court. In 14 of the 80 cases in which probation was recommended, forms of probation other than the Driver Retraining Scheme have been followed. This arises when, for example, a defendant already has a full driving licence. It has also occurred when a defendant is convicted of excess alcohol and disqualification is mandatory. There have been few such cases and these have generally involved older defendants. The only other exclusions have been one defendant who was already disqualified for a lengthy period, and another who was medically unfit to hold a driving licence.

The scheme makes use of a short probation order of nine months' duration as the basis for the programme. Each course lasts approximately six months, this being the approximate waiting time for driving tests in London. The nine-month order gives flexibility, which is needed because some clients may have to wait before starting their course since each group of between nine and twelve clients takes up to two months to be assembled. At the termination of a course, the probation orders are discharged if the client has carried out the programme and is not awaiting sentence for any subsequent conviction.

Magistrates have agreed to avoid imposing disqualification on clients placed on probation to participate in driver retraining, although defendants do receive the eight points on their licences which have replaced endorsement under the 1981 Transport Act. Where there are multiple offences, each carrying penalty points, the points are not added up but operate concurrently with the offence gaining the greatest number of points defining the maximum points liability on a licence.

The result for defendants is that disqualification is avoided, although with eight points on their licences they have to take great care to avoid subsequent traffic offences which would take them up to, or over, the 12 points permitted before disqualification is generally imposed under the 'totting-up' procedure. Additionally, defendants avoid at least a fine and at worst a custodial sentence. Staff estimate that it costs a client between £80 and £100 to carry out the Driver Retraining programme in paying for a provisional licence, test fee and, say, ten driving lessons. Such a sum compares favourably with the levels of fines which are typical even for unemployed defendants. Clients generally perceive the deal of driver retraining as fair and reasonable.

Prior to a recommendation being made for driver retraining, it is clearly and carefully explained to clients that their agreement to being placed on probation is necessary, and that this agreement commits them to participating in the scheme. It is made clear that the clients should:

1 apply for a provisional driving licence;
2 apply for a driving test within the first month of the start of the course;
3 take sufficient driving lessons at a driving school of the clients' choice to enable them to have a reasonable chance of passing the test;
4 take the driving test on the booked date;
5 observe the normal conditions of probation with regard to avoiding further offending, reporting as instructed, seeking and retaining employment, and notifying changes of address and employment.

Clients are expected to pay for licences, tests and driving lessons themselves, whether or not they are in employment. Although this can be difficult for unemployed clients, many such clients manage to afford it, sometimes with parental support, through changing their spending priorities. It is made clear to clients that persistent failure to report and participate in the scheme, as well as reoffending, are breaches of probation, and that after due warning failure to report regularly will result in a return to court.

Clients are seen individually, usually each week, prior to the start of a course. Help is given in making applications for provisional licences and driving tests, and with other matters as needed. Some clients are involved with the activities of the 'Newheels Motor Project' by this stage and participate in weekend and evening activities such as motor-cycle scrambling, banger-racing and mechanics. These practical activities form a voluntary part of the programme and attract some, but by no means all, clients.

The course itself consists of between 14 and 18 meetings spread over a six-month period, the number depending on such matters as the progress and needs of each particular group. Initially meetings take place weekly in the evenings to permit those at work to attend. Once a group becomes established, the frequency of meetings changes to fortnightly, with a gap of three weeks around the middle of the course. Weekly meetings are resumed for the last month, leading up to the time when most members of the group take the driving test. Due to the way the test centres operate, it is not possible for all group members to take their tests at the same time. Moreover, as test dates approach, some group members cancel their tests and receive later dates as it becomes clear to them and their driving instructors that they are not yet ready for the test.

The size of groups is of some importance and each has started with between nine and twelve clients. This size makes allowance for potential drop-outs. Staff feel that six regular group members is the lowest needed to enable a group to remain viable. Different probation officers seem to feel comfortable with varying numbers, and the size of groups has ranged between six and ten members, a typical number being nine clients after one or two clients have dropped out. Each session lasts approximately 1½ hours and each course is jointly led by two probation officers. To date, each pair has consisted of a man and a woman officer, but earlier groups were jointly led by two male officers and there seems no reason why group leaders should not be of the same sex.

A detailed programme has been developed with materials available for each session. The main focus of the work done in the group sessions is educative. The 'syllabus' is derived from a range of materials, such as the Highway Code and other literature on motoring practice, some appropriately altered materials from American 'defensive driving' training, and materials pertaining to insurance requirements and law, safety, roadcraft, car purchase, and offending behaviour. Various educative techniques are employed, including quizzes, lectures, films, role-plays, homework exercises (e.g. obtaining insurance quotations), and video. Talks and demonstrations are provided by traffic police officers of the Metropolitan Police Force, such as procedures to be followed in an accident, breathalysers, etc. Towards the end of each course, a film of the driving test is shown, followed by discussions with a former driving test examiner at a local road safety centre. Videos of 'commentary driving' made by probation officers at the Unit are also shown. Staff also spend some of the sessions exploring the clients' offending behaviour as related to cars, with emphasis being placed on learning more effective ways of handling group pressure to offend, and such issues as opportunity and risk. Use is made of videotaping in carrying out this part of the course, which often includes disclosure of clients' undetected previous offending.

The materials used in each session give purpose to, and stimulate discussion within, the group and they also provide information for the clients. Having structured materials available also seems to increase the group leaders' confidence. Whilst materials have been continually developed and tried out with various groups, the programme is not followed mechanically and the order and style of the material can be freely adapted to suit the needs of each particular group. This is necessary when, for example, a group contains a number of illiterate clients and written material therefore has to be verbally and pictorially adapted. Group leaders also draw on their own knowledge and experience of driving and, whilst they do not have to be advanced motorists, an interest in driving as a skill is obviously useful.

In earlier groups, about half of the clients actually took the test, with only half of these passing first time. In one group all the clients 'bottled out' despite having booked a test date! Something which has emerged with some clients is a reluctance to have their driving tested. For a few clients, as will be discussed below, this is because they discover they are no longer interested in driving. However, for many, the problem is one of gaining sufficient driving experience. There is no easy solution to this difficulty as the cost of lessons is high, and the majority of clients do not have access to cars in the family on which to practise. Off-road driving experience is of little value and relevance to actual driving.

The experience of operating the scheme

The comments in this section are based on the experience of the seven groups which have been run to date, involving 66 clients and six probation officers. There has been no independent evaluation of the opinions of those involved. However, officers running the courses have talked with magistrates and have attempted to evaluate each course with its members.

As has already been suggested, the scheme is popular with sentencers. Recommendations for probation where driver retraining was specified were followed in 93 per cent of cases. Courts have also exercised their discretion in avoiding disqualification and, following discussions, sentencers recognize the cost of the scheme to the client by keeping fines to a minimum.

For the six officers who have run the courses, the principal challenge has lain in their having to depart from their more usual style of work with individuals and instead work in a structured group setting. General opinion has been that once this difficulty has been tackled the scheme does provide officers with the confidence to recommend probation more frequently for TDA offenders. A major factor in helping the officers has been the apparent relevance of the scheme as evidenced in the clients' response. Attendance at the weekly groups has been consistently high, which would appear to indicate a level of interest and commitment not always found with clients coming within a similar age range. An average of eight out of ten clients who start the course finish it, and the drop-out usually happens very early on. Drop-out typically occurs with clients who fail to attend initial groups and are therefore breached and returned to court. Experience so far shows that 90 per cent of clients taking part in the programme obtain their provisional driving licences, and half of these will have booked and paid for their tests during the first half of a course. Success rates in tests are, of course, much lower for those making their first attempt. However, around 50 per cent of those taking the test pass first time: a proportion similar to that of the general population.

Also important for the probation officers running the scheme is its flexibility. Through concentrating on the offence, it has proved possible to accommodate clients for whom it had been believed that their theft of motor vehicles was simply the result of the desire to drive, but for whom it was discovered subsequently that a general lack of self-confidence was central. In such cases, tests have often been postponed or cancelled in favour of pursuing some other goal. For instance, a number succeeded in finding work, while others have participated in activities like banger-racing, or completely different pursuits such as those provided by 'Operation Drake'.

When clients speak for themselves, their comments have suggested to staff that the scheme has met their needs and lived up to their expectations. Asked if they had understood from the outset what Driver Retraining was about, and why they had opted for it, typical replies have been: 'Nearly all of it matched up to what you said'; 'It seemed the best opportunity to keep driving'; 'It was either lose my licence or do DRS.'

However, sometimes there was misunderstanding as to how much probation officers would be responsible for actual driving instruction, for example: 'I thought you were going to teach us to drive ... when you gave us the list of driving schools I realized you weren't.'

Speaking about the content of the course generally, typical remarks were: 'It teaches you everything about driving'; 'It's a legal way to get your licence'; 'You learn something from it'; 'I've put off doing anything about my driving. This course gives me the push I needed'; 'It probably does get you nearer a test.'

Comments were frequently made about specific components of the course, for example: 'You know what to expect when you get nicked again'; 'It's not worth getting nicked again' (relating to a sentencing exercise where clients were placed in the magistrate's role to consider TDA offences); 'The Road Safety Centre was the best bit'; 'Once you see the film the test doesn't seem too bad' (relating to an instructor at the 'City Driving Centre' showing a film of a driving test). The majority of clients also referred to the importance of the course for enabling them to learn the Highway Code.

Most clients felt that by the end of the course their attitudes to driving had improved. For one client the course 'makes you think about taking precautions'. The most frequent references made concerned the new skills learned and the technical information imparted from the course.

Staff were particularly concerned about whether meeting as a group had proved inhibiting for clients. No one saw this as a problem, and most clients said it was an advantage. One remarked: 'It's better in a group. It's a bit like Mastermind being on you own.' Asked to explain what he meant by this, this young man said that seeing a probation officer in an office made him feel as though he was being interrogated.

For those clients, referred to earlier, who discovered that driving was of little real importance, rather different opinions were expressed. Nonetheless, the importance of the group setting remained: 'Since coming here I don't think about driving any more'; 'I like coming to see the others'; 'What else is there to do on a Tuesday?'

Conclusions

A full evaluation of the scheme was undertaken in 1984, after the development sample had all completed their courses. The conclusions made in this paper are drawn from this evaluation as well as from earlier work.

The objectives of the scheme can be summarized as follows:

1 to extend the use of the probation order with TDA offenders, and specifically with those having two and more previous convictions;
2 to avoid disqualification from driving being imposed on TDA offenders, through offering the courts a positive alternative in sentencing;
3 to assist TDA offenders in taking practical steps to legitimize their driving and, in the case of TDA offenders for whom driving is only of marginal interest, to provide other approaches still using a probation order;
4 to develop the attitude amongst offenders that driving is a responsible and skilled activity;
5 to develop social work techniques encouraging offenders to avoid opportunities to commit autocrime.

The first and second of these objectives have been achieved, in that the recommendation rate for probation orders concerning TDA offenders has been raised from around 20 per cent to over 73 per cent; and courts have followed such recommendations at a consistently high rate averaging out at 83 per cent. Courts have also exercised their discretion in avoiding disqualification for all but one case so far. It has also been demonstrated that it is practicable to use probation for TDA offenders who, prior to the scheme, may have received custodial sentences. The net effect has been substantially to increase the use of the probation order in managing this particular group of offenders within the community.

The scheme also assists clients to take steps towards legitimizing their driving, and offers a positive and focused method of supervising them. The high levels of clients' response to and interest in the scheme, as demonstrated by their regular attendance at sessions, suggests that the objectives of the scheme are seen as relevant by clients. From observation and the comments of clients, it is evident that their driving knowledge and ability substantially increase in the course of the programme. Even when clients do not take the test, or postpone it, it is unlikely that they have not benefited at all from the programme, which may have restrained them from committing further offences.

Of the 66 clients who started the course, 59 effectively took part, and nearly all of these completed the scheme. Of the other seven, four never started, reoffending very early on. During the course of the probation order (approximately nine months), 18 clients reoffended, i.e. 27 per cent. Two-thirds of these, however, continued on probation despite the reconviction. The reconviction rate at 12 months was 33 per cent, and over two years a total of 35 clients (53 per cent) have been reconvicted of a 'standard list' offence. What was striking was the fact that only six of the reconvictions, over two years, were for offences of TDA, i.e. less than 10 per cent.

The results were, in fact, better than expected given the nature of the clients. They were all young men, under the age of 23, and 85 per cent of them had previous convictions, the mean number of previous convictions being four. For those with previous convictions, over 60 per cent had convictions for TDA prior to the conviction which resulted in the probation order. We would have expected 12-month reconviction rates to have been between 40 per cent and 50 per cent and two-year rates to have been in excess of 60 per cent. The observed reconviction rates were lower than expected, and the incidence of 'repeat offending', i.e for TDA, was very low at 10 per cent.

The vast majority of the 59 clients who participated in the scheme applied for, and obtained, provisional driving licences. Over 30 clients applied for the driving test, although only 21 actually took it, of whom 12 passed first time. As mentioned above, a number of clients 'bottled out' of their tests and many of these had insufficiently prepared themselves through not having enough driving lessons.

The experience of the scheme has been an encouraging one. Driver Retraining does appear to go some way towards meeting its main objective, that of managing the TDA offender in the community with what appears to have been a more positive, and certainly less expensive, outcome than custody. This approach has now been absorbed within mainstream field units in the North-East Division of ILPS and is now available to courts throughout that area.

5

Centre 81: Clients' and Officers' Views on the Southampton Day Centre

Richard Hil

Introduction

During a conference held in June 1979 to discuss a House of Commons Expenditure Committee report, the Chief Probation Officer of Devon, Mr Roy Bailey, stated that: 'Day Centres are a major priority for the Probation Service at the present time if it is to demonstrate to the courts that it has available the non-custodial facilities to be able to successfully contain and care for offenders who might otherwise go to prison' (Bailey, 1979). It is largely a matter of speculation as to how far Day Centres, Day Training Centres and the whole train of 'custodial alternatives' actually divert offenders from prison. However, this paper is based on the informed assumption that offenders would probably be committed to custody if Day Centres did not exist, such facilities thereby serving as alternatives for a 'potentially divertible' band of offenders for whom 'prison is a real but not inevitable possibility' (Bottoms and McWilliams, 1979, 180). Such offenders include petty thieves and burglars, vagrants, drunks and social inadequates. This paper conveys the views and attitudes of clients and officers in regard to Centre 81. It sets out a brief history of the Centre which clearly illustrates that the creation of a 'custodial alternative' is far from an easy or clear-cut process.

Centre 81 opened in September 1980, and is staffed by a senior probation officer, five main grade officers, an ancillary,

and secretarial staff. A number of voluntary associates have
also been recruited on a part-time basis. Despite considerable
staff turnover, the composition of the Day Centre team has not
changed. The Centre is located in a block of grey-green
buildings on the outskirts of Southampton city centre. The
building, which once housed the Hampshire Constabulary
Fraud Squad, stands across the road from the new redbrick
complex of the main Southampton probation office. Office
accommodation, secretarial help, record keeping and client
supervision are shared, and the caseload is distributed on a
collective rather than individual basis. The team caseload in
November 1981 was 250 and has risen steadily to 360 in
August 1982. The average caseload for main grade officers is
54.

The Centre offers a number of facilities including a coffee
bar, books, magazines, newspapers, playing cards, chess, etc.
Games such as pool, table tennis and darts are popular among
the clients. 'Clean-up' facilities such as shaving, soap and a
razor supply are available, as well as a stock of second-hand
clothing (provided by a local dry cleaner) and a washing
machine.

The Centre has rooms available for one-to-one interviews
with clients. For those who are unable to attend during the
day, a common reporting night has been arranged by the
team. The Centre is also used by Southampton probation
officers for various group activities, such as the community
group in which clients are encouraged to air their views, the
Tuesday Club (for 'social isolates'), the sex offenders' group,
the prisoners' wives' groups, support and self-help group
(SASH: for female offenders who find it hard to cope with
families and other demands) and an activities group for
'monosyllabic offenders'. The Centre's staff also have contacts
with a number of outside bodies, such as the Society of St
Dismas (for alcoholics), the Wessex Council on Alcoholism,
the Department of Psychiatry at the South Hampshire Hospital, the Church Army, Salvation Army, Welfare Rights Office

and various accommodation agencies dealing with hostels and other forms of residence. The Centre 81 team has proposed – but has yet to establish – an induction group for new clients, a welfare rights bureau and a claimants' union.

Establishing priorities: a parochial history of Centre 81

The Southampton Day Centre has its roots in the reorganisation of the Southampton probation and after-care office in 1975. From this it became widely felt that some reappraisal of the traditional reliance on one-to-one office-based work was necessary. In particular, it was recognized that certain clients could benefit from groupwork activities.

Although both field officers and management were aware of the need to develop new methods of social work, it was argued that office policy should be based on evidence about client 'need'. Moreover, as management observed, the Southampton office 'had no point of focus. A lot of people were pursuing their own ends ... There was a lack of unified policy or purpose and a great deal of low morale. It was all very destructive for officers.'

In response to this situation, the Southampton office decided to mount an investigation into workloads and caseloads. The proposal for an office working party was made in the summer of 1977 following a number of meetings between Hampshire management and Southampton senior officers. With the encouragement of management and consent of officers, a Working Party on Objectives (WPO) was set up in the autumn of 1977. Its terms of reference were:

1 To formulate long-term strategies and objectives for the office;
2 to collect information on work patterns;
3 to present a write-up to be combined with a review.

Around this time the issue of 'decentralization' emerged. Briefly, it was argued by management that the Southampton office should be split into 'village-based' units. This was based on two arguments: first, probation officers could work more effectively on a localized basis, and second, the modern Southampton office complex was 'too expensive to run'. The decentralization proposal ran into strong opposition from field officers in Southampton and many felt they had not been adequately informed about details of the proposal. The key objections were that the Southampton office was a convenient, central place for clients and that group activities could not be easily organized in a small, local office. Despite the controversy surrounding the decentralization issue it proved to be constructive in providing another reason for scrutinizing the Southampton work/caseload.

In session one of WPO (October 1977), the objectives of the proposed investigations were further clarified: 'we need to research the effectiveness of our work with clients and look at categories such as sex/age, number of previous convictions, types of offences, previous court appearances, institutional backgrounds, areas of the city, etc.' In a later session (November 1977), it was argued that even if the office were to be 'divided up' (a reference to decentralization) there was still a need to 'clarify its objectives'. These objectives were closely tied in with a general consideration of the role of the probation service. For example, it was maintained that any discussion on 'effectiveness' would have to be preceded by reference to broader penological and social work issues. Was the service in the business of 'helping people to function more satisfactorily', or 'preventing recidivisim', or was it simply an 'agency of social control'? These and other questions were discussed at the second WPO during which some of the major aims of the service were identified: 'the prevention of further offending', 'keeping people out of prison', 'changing people', 'enabling people to improve the quality of their lives', 'helping people to survive' and even 'promoting social change'.

Constructing a Day Centre 'philosophy'

By 'philosophy' we refer loosely to the attempt to systematize knowledge and ideas into a coherent and practical method of working. Since 1975 the theory and practice of various social work methods has been under review. Although much of the discussion was vague, it became clear that the concern of the probation service, according to WPO, was orientated around 'help' and 'care' rather than 'treatment', 'therapy' or 'reintegration'. It was argued moreover that, if adequate provision were available, a number of young offenders could be diverted from custody. The working party covered a three-month period in detail and found that in only 25 per cent of cases where a social inquiry report was prepared did officers refer to custodial alternatives for young offenders. These findings reinforced the feeling that new and credible alternatives to imprisonment should be established and presented to the courts.

The core of the Day Centre philosophy stemmed from the fact that the Southampton caseload was made up of a considerable number of offenders with overlapping problems of alcoholism, social isolation and unemployment. These people could not be adequately supervised in a one-to-one office-based situation. It was agreed that a day-care context would offer a more appropriate setting for protracted supervision.

In an effort to establish priorities for the Centre, a team of officers met in May 1979 for a three-day planning discussion. The aim was to assess the needs of 165 designated clients. The client group was broken down according to age, sex, previous convictions and type of supervision. Various problem areas were identified including isolation, drink, drugs, family relations, unemployment, sexual deviation, violence and delinquency. The team then discussed social work methods such as one-to-one counselling, 'drop-in' facilities and groupwork. A list was drawn up to set priorities for facilities and work methods. The emphasis throughout this exercise was on administrative matters such as organizing recording tasks and rota duties. Basic decisions were taken in regard to the organization and use of the accommodation. Interestingly, only three groups were given a major priority for Centre work: the social isolates group, painting and decoration group, and the wives' group; five groups were given secondary priority: literacy/numeracy, life skills, employment, drinkers, relatives. This early prioritization was regarded by the team as tentative groundwork for future work within the Centre. Indeed, a pragmatic approach was seen as the best way to respond to changing circumstances and needs.

Inside-out: the clients' view of Centre 81

This section is based on two samples: 15 clients interviewed in June/July 1980 and 25 clients in May/June 1982. All 40 respondents were in the 17–21 age range. This age group make up about 55 to 60 per cent of the Day Centre clientele at any one time. Typically, the Day Centre client is single, male and on a probation order or Borstal licence. He is unemployed and has no educational qualifications. He has a record of petty offences such as theft, burglary, and/or TDA. He is likely to have experienced detention centres, Borstals and, in some cases, prison. The client attends the Centre for either half-a-day or a full day per week along with two or three others. It is unlikely that female clients will be present. The following extracts represent views expressed in both samples.

Conceptual images

Well over half of the combined sample felt that if attendance at the Centre was purely voluntary they would not attend. A fairly typical remark was: 'I also tend to view the centre in terms of control and punishment.' As one client put it: 'Let's face it, this place is about punishment, isn't it? ... We've got to attend and behave according to the rules ... There aren't any locks or chains but we've still got keepers.' Another client remarked: 'The officers claim to do a lot of things but as far as I'm concerned they're here to keep us under control.' During the course of the research it became clear that length of attendance had an influence on the client's view of the Centre, particularly if successful relations were built up with the staff. Thus many clients changed their description of the Centre from emphasizing 'control' and 'punishment' to 'warmth', 'understanding' and 'friendship'. In general, however, clients perceived the Centre in terms of help, care *and* control. These elements were regarded as interconnected and numerous clients stated that the official control function of officers was compatible with care and help. Typical is the client who remarked:

It's pretty clear what this place is about ... There's no doubt that the officers keep us in order and supervise us ... That's their job isn't it, to keep us under some kind of legal control? On the other hand though, I think they do a good job in helping a lot of people here particularly with practical matters such as getting dole money or accommodation but they also help us with other things like helping us to calm down and getting us to learn to communicate properly ... I'd say they've helped me a lot in that sort of way; you know, by persuading me that smacking someone first and talking later isn't always the best policy. (20-year-old probationer)

Generally clients viewed the Centre in positive, relational terms with the control element as a necessary counterpart to help and care. As another client put it: 'I think most people who attend this place tend to see it as a combination of supervision and control and help and understanding' (young prisoner licensee, aged 21).

Custody versus non-custody

When contrasting the experience of custody with Centre 81, clients invariably stated that in a Day Centre it was possible to 'talk about problems' with officers who were 'prepared to listen'. Most clients regarded this as a major attribute of the Centre, as the following extracts illustrate:

It's a lot different [from detention centre] 'cos if you had a problem inside they just didn't want to know. But here you can come and talk to your probation officer ... It makes a big difference ... At least they treat you like a human being ... You can talk things out with them and they'll help you if you've got a problem or something. (detention centre licensee, aged 19)

Probation Officers listen better than the screws do ... They give you a straight answer, the screw won't ... It's good to know that an officer will listen and help if he can ... It's not like that inside. (Borstal licensee, aged 20)

When you're inside you're restricted in what you can say ... but here you've got the opportunity to talk things out ... You can say whether it's bad or good or whatever ... People listen to you ... whether they can do anything is another question [laughter] ... At least they listen ... Even though it's a probation office you still get a good atmosphere and can talk freely ... It means a lot to me to say something straight ... You can't do that in Borstal, it just causes problems ... When you're inside the screws never listen to you ... It's all about punishment ... Here you can tell your problems freely but inside they're forced out of you. (Borstal licensee, aged 20)

Clients tended to characterize the Centre as 'warm' and 'caring', and contrasted this with the 'cold', 'uncaring', 'brutal' and even 'cruel' experience of custody. Not surprisingly, the vast majority of respondents felt that detention centres and Borstals were personally destructive and ineffective, particularly as far as preventing further offending was concerned. There was a great deal of hostility and resentment towards such institutions.

The social skills 'spin-off'

At least half of the combined sample stated that the Centre had some impact on their social behaviour. For many clients the experience of conversing with officials was novel. As one client remarked:

I suppose it's the first time I've been able to talk to someone in authority so openly and honestly. It's done me a tremendous amount of good because I've been able to listen to advice and learn things about myself . . . I've definitely benefited from the experience. I'm a lot calmer now. I'd prefer to talk things out rather than belt someone. (Borstal licensee, aged 21)

Day care and traditional office-based work

The vast majority of clients felt that the benefits of day care far outweighed those of the traditional office-based, one-to-one situation. The following account is typical:

It's a joke the other way; you know (in the traditional setting) . . . You sit around in some pokey corridor waiting for about half 'n hour for the officer who then asks you a few questions about employment prospects or accommodation 'n' that . . . But you get the feeling that he doesn't give a toss; you know, he just wants you to get out of the place . . . In the Day Centre it's different, more relaxed, people have got time for you and they treat you like a human being . . . It's a lot better. (Borstal licensee, aged 19)

Another client remarked:

Well, there's no comparison is there? . . . I mean, before, they didn't give a toss . . . I used to get pretty angry because I could see he wasn't interested and that he just wanted to get off . . . They ask you stupid questions which are more in the way of prying into your life rather than trying to really help you out . . . Yes, I'd say it's a lot better in the Centre . . . They seem to have the time to listen to you and they don't mind giving some friendly and worthwhile advice . . . I feel a great degree of attachment to this place than I ever did before. (Borstal licensee, aged 20)

Although Centre 81 officers advocate a less one-to-one orientated system, rooms in the Centre are still retained for purposes of induction and private interviews. However, there are few of the rigidities which accompany traditional office-based interviews. Clients clearly prefer the Day Centre setting, particularly when compared to traditional casework.

'Off the street?'

In answer to the question of what clients would be doing if the Centre were not open, most stated that they would be 'wandering around the streets', 'watching telly', 'playing records', 'cycling round town' or spending their time 'in the library', 'in the pub' or 'at the bookies', or, as in one case, 'screwing the missus'. Most clients stated that attendance at the Centre had prevented them from further offending, as the following extracts indicate:

It's kept me out of trouble ... I can't afford that ... so I come up here and pass the time. Otherwise I'd just be mucking around the streets creating trouble with me mates ... Now if I get bored I come up here and talk to a probation officer or play a game and then up home ... It helps to keep me out of trouble. (Borstal licensee, aged 19)

It's alright here ... It keeps you out of trouble ... If you're on the dole and can't get a job it gives you something to do ... You can come in when you like ... If I didn't come here I'd be sitting at home getting bored stiff; boredom drives me mad ... I suppose I'll get in trouble sometime because once I leave here I'll get bored and start looking for excitement. (probationer, aged 21)

For the time it's open it gives me something to do, somewhere to go ... I just come in and talk to my officer or whoever is about, perhaps I'll have a game of pool, but it's comforting to know that you can come here without getting all the dirty looks that you do say in a cafe or pub. (probationer, aged 20)

Since attending the Centre, only a small number of clients have reappeared before the courts. Although there are no accurate figures on reconviction rates among Day Centre attenders nationally, an analysis of Centre 81 files indicates a reoffending rate of 10 per cent among clients while attending the Centre. Thus, for a short period, the Centre appears to act as a brake on offending.

The assertion by clients that attendance at the Centre kept them 'off the streets' should be viewed with caution, particularly since the average level of attendance is about a half to one full day per week. This means that most time is spent away from the Centre. Moreover, the opportunity for attending the Centre is severely limited by the fact that it is open only 3½ days per week and closes altogether at weekends. This makes the term 'Day Centre' appear a little hollow. One client summed up his feelings on this topic as follows:

Well, its bloody farcical really, isn't it?! A Day Centre they call it, more like a part-time Day Centre ... The place should at least be open on the Saturday or even Sunday when a lot of people tend to get into trouble because they're bored out of their skulls ... But at worst the place should be open five days a week – it doesn't even do that. And even on the full days the Centre shuts for one hour during the lunch break. We're turfed out. Crazy isn't it?. (probationer, 21 years old)

Outside the Centre the clients generally pay visits to the DHSS, pubs, bookmakers or simply 'hang around' or 'do nothing'. A small number of clients attend for 2½ days or more a week. Like other clients they refer to the Centre as a respite from the boredom of 'sitting at home' or 'hanging around the streets'. For these people the Centre did have a more significant part to play in occupying their time. However, for most clients the weekends were particularly problematic since the Centre is shut and they do not possess the necessary cash to enjoy weekend activities. As one remarked:

I'd really like to come here at weekends. If you've got no money on a Saturday you just sort of hang around the Centre staring at people going by. Great fun eh? Can't even go to the match ... Sunday's even worse. I feel like toppin' meself sometimes ... That's when you

82   RICHARD HIL

really need company and somewhere to go especially if you've got no money. I mean, entertainment costs a lot of bread. (probationer, 20 years old)

Down at the DHSS

In a reference to the 'continuing hassles with the Department of Health and Social Security', a recent team review noted that: 'Work on the above issue is important but detracts from working positively and creatively in the Centre.' As far as the clients are concerned, the endless representations made by officers to the DHSS constitute perhaps the most important aspect of help. As one client put it: 'my probation officer is a great help when it comes to dealing with the DHSS. They can be a right pain in the arse.' (probationer, 19 years old).

For those who are unemployed – this accounts for 87 per cent of all Day Centre users – the issue of supplementary benefit payouts is emotionally charged, particularly since for some it becomes a matter of survival:

'We get to rely on officers to battle for us because the SS don't give a fuck ... You know ... they shunt us in and out as quickly as possible ... They make me sick ... The officers do a great job for us and without them some of the blokes would be right in the shit ... We all need money for the basic necessities. (probationer, 18 years old)

My probation officer's been great to me ... especially in getting money out of the dole office. It can be a real pain sometimes ... you have to wait and fill in forms and go to interviews and you still end up getting the wrong amount of cash ... Can drive you fuckin' mad it can ... My officer just gets on the phone and tries to sort things out ... it might take a lot of shoutin' but eventually they come up with the goods. (probationer, 20 years old)

The Centre has a welfare rights noticeboard which includes information on how to go about claiming welfare benefits.

Some clients argue that they would rather attend specialist classes to 'demystify' claiming procedures. Others have complained about the lack of knowledge regarding welfare rights among probation officers. However, it appears that most clients eventually obtain their entitlements from the DHSS even though they often feel harrassed, abused and stigmatized in the process.

Groupwork

Generally groups within the Centre are poorly attended. During the research for this paper, 17 clients were asked whether they had been informed of groupwork activity in the Centre: eight said no and nine said yes. Of the nine who had knowledge of the groups, only one chose to attend. A reason for this lack of response to groupwork is that many people feel there should be more 'practical' activities such as occupational therapy, leisure groups, photography, motorcycle and motor-vehicle maintenance, literacy and numeracy classes. At present groupwork appeals to only a small number of clients and there is little to cater for those individuals who wish to learn skills and activities which might strengthen their position in a heavily depressed job market.

There's nothing going on here if you really want to learn something. You can learn how to play darts, drink coffee or play chess but what's the good of that in the real world. (Borstal licensee, aged 19 years)

I would like to learn something practical which might be of some help in getting a job ... I feel I'm wasting my life here in many ways ... I could be learning something useful. (detention centre licensee, aged 18 years)

The Day Centre is more like a bloody cafe! They don't teach you anything practical here, it's all silly games and pastimes ... waste of time really. (probationer, aged 19 years)

Powerlessness

A particular point of issue among some clients is the lack of participation in the organization and management of the Centre. Despite a fortnightly community group, which meets to air views about the Centre, there appears to be little or no opportunity for clients to make decisions which might influence the way it is run. As one subject put it: 'We get no say in the running of this place and that only reinforces the view that we're people who need to be supervised.' Some officers argue that clients are unable to articulate their feelings in the group situation, an argument which, if taken seriously, would challenge the very 'philosophy' of the Centre. Clients recognize the difficulties experienced in group settings yet, as one Borstal licensee put it: 'If this place is run for our benefit then we should have some say in how it's run ... It stands to reason, doesn't it?'

Despite frequent complaints of 'boredom', alienation and lack of influence, clients view the Centre essentially in positive terms. They describe it in terms of help and care, although the control element is seen as a major, but not incompatible, function.

The most vivid contrast made with custody was that in the Centre there was always 'someone to talk to'. Detention centres, Borstals and prisons were perceived as brutalizing institutions in which personal problems remained undiscussed and unresolved. In contrast, clients felt encouraged to articulate their thoughts and feelings to officials who were prepared to listen and help. For many, this was a novel experience. Generally, the Centre was thought of as a useful and constructive departure from traditional casework and a meaningful alternative to the custodial experience.

Day-care supervision: the officers' view

Social work in a day-care context poses far more problems and demands on officers than traditional office-based supervision.

One of the major problems is the attitude of field officers towards the form of work undertaken by Centre 81 staff. As one Day Centre officer remarked:

The suspicion is with us all the time. The team . . . had to go it alone . . . They had to make a go of it . . . Many officers felt there was too much of an elitist air about the Centre team and this provoked some hostility. It's lessened a bit now and the Day Centre is seen as part of the Southampton office.

Day-care officers also face a host of practical and emotional pressures imposed by lengthy periods of supervision. For example, whereas an office-based interview is a relatively short and formal affair, day-centre supervision involves creating and sustaining workable relations with clients over a long period. Given this, the ability to establish friendships is crucial and some officers are more capable than others of achieving this in practice.

Defining the Day Centre

Despite the team's emphasis on providing help and care for a hybrid group of socially isolated, inadequate, alcoholic and unemployed clients, there was no general agreement concerning the specific purpose of the Centre. This, in part, is due to the fact that the Centre's clientele is composed of a majority group of young offenders who appear to suffer the disadvantages of a criminal record and unemployment. Significantly, only a small number of sample members suffered from any other problems and these tended to be problems of accommodation and finance rather than 'social isolation' or 'inadequacy'. Indeed, it was often difficult to understand why some clients attended the Centre at all, since their problems were no different from the problems of those who continued to receive traditional office-based supervision. Somewhat surprisingly, the Centre team has made no real effort to identify a 'core group' of clients who suffer from overlapping problems of isolation, inadequacy and unemployment. Obviously, some 'core' clients are easier to identify than others (e.g. the

alcoholics and homeless) but many of the younger clients
would not appear to fit such simple categories.

The lack of clear definition concerning the exact purpose of
the Centre is reflected in the different descriptions provided
by Centre 81 officers. Thus it was variously referred to as, 'a
probation detention centre', 'a residential centre', 'a group
setting', 'an accommodation resource', 'a community-based
scheme' and 'a team approach to supervision'. Some officers
place emphasis on two or more of these definitions and others
used only a single description. All officers, however, qualified
their statements by referring to the importance of identifying
client problems and developing appropriate social work
methods to deal with them. This exercise has yet to be carried
out. The absence of a clear definition concerns some officers,
who criticized the team's 'lack of direction' and the problem of
having 'no clearly delineated aims' in their work with clients.
Problems of this kind reduce morale and confidence, and it is
not surprising that the development of new social work
methods and schemes within the Centre has stultified.

'Back-door intervention'

The purpose of the Centre has been described by one officer as
follows:

Care is an important part of our work; it helps to create an
environment where clients can be accepted and learn acceptable
standards of behaviour. The reason why people commit offences is
often because they're isolated and drunk etc. If there's a place where
they can have contact with others it might help to keep them off the
streets ... Although it's in an indirect way that we try to deal with
re-offending ... we try to tackle the causes rather than the symp-
toms. If you agree that people are more acceptable than their
criminality suggests, then you don't have to spend all your time
talking about crime ... They know the pros and cons already ... we
try to get at the cause – it's a backdoor entrance but it's the only
approach that has relevance ... We look at the reasons why people

get into trouble ... If we do that then perhaps we can bring about a long term rather than short term change.

In various ways the Centre 81 team has adopted this social work orientation and, as has been suggested, many clients seem to have benefited in both personal and relational terms. By encouraging clients to articulate their thoughts and feelings, officers have been able to discourage aggressive outbursts which previously landed them in trouble with the police.

Self-determination

While the team has developed a supportive atmosphere within the Centre, it is stressed that the onus for personal problem-solving lies with the client. As one officer put it:

I don't set out to change lifestyles ... I think we offer people the opportunity to progress and it's up to them whether they take the opportunity ... Not everyone is ready for that when they come here but they have the facilities to help themselves ... It's more about giving them space and help so they can cope with the practical difficulties of living.

The emphasis on client self-determination has been brought about, in part, by the fear of creating dependence on the Centre. As one officer remarked: 'We fear dependency occurring among our clients ... It's incumbent upon us to prepare people for that ... We may have to wean people off the Centre'.

This dependence is evidenced by the fact that many clients frequently visit the Centre once their orders have expired. For many, the prospect of departure is an unhappy one; they feel they are being put 'back on the streets' without any appreciable change in their social or economic circumstances. Officers see departure as a 'hit-and-miss' affair or even a retrograde step: 'We're not too sure what they're going to do once they leave the Centre ... They could make it by getting a job or

settling down with a girl or they could end up back in court.
There's no way of knowing.'

Images of day care social work

The majority of officers view the Centre in terms of helping
clients to make 'specific changes' in their 'lifestyles' and 'social
behaviour'. There was a surprising degree of similarity between clients' and officers' views in regard to the overall aims
and objectives of Centre 81. Both placed emphasis on the
traditional triad of 'advising, assisting and befriending', these
being perceived as the basis of work and relationships within
the Centre. Clients asserted a close interconnection between
help, care, and control: the latter element was seen as a
complementary aspect of help and care. Likewise, officers saw
the principal task in terms of providing help and care but,
equally, the control function inherent in the probation order
was seen as an indispensable part of client supervision. 'After all,'
as one officer put it, 'we're officers of the court and it's our job
to ensure the requirements of the order are carried out to the
last letter. Hopefully, we are also able to match this control
element with the provision of help and care. It's a balancing
job which I think we do quite successfully'.

According to probation officers, Centre 81 is firmly based
on principles of companionship, help, care and containment.
This more or less corresponds with the clients' view, although
they regard control as a more explicit feature of the Centre.

While advocating a 'back–door approach' to client supervision, officers have experienced severe difficulties in building
up adequate resources and activities to cope with client needs.
Moreover, despite the recruitment of voluntary associates and
extensive links with outside agencies, officers have not come to
terms with the nature of their workload. This inevitably
affects the level of client contact. Data gathered on officers'
workloads showed that most time was spent in routine administrative activities and only a small proportion of time in
direct contact with clients (Hil, 1980). Other tasks such as

prison visits and court duties left officers with very little time to develop initiatives within the Centre. These pressures have meant that some of the most basic aims and plans of the Centre have not been realized.

Towards a conclusion

The paper began by focusing on the creation of Centre 81. The Centre was established, and continues to function, on a pragmatic basis with emphasis being placed on 'help' and 'care' rather than on 'treatment' or 'therapy'. Such an emphasis does little to reduce the incidence of post-programme offending, and does not help at all with regard to other major problems faced by clients, such as unemployment and shortage of money.

Despite such shortcomings, it is clear that clients appreciate the help offered by officers, particularly in respect of obtaining supplementary benefit payments. However, many clients argue that the Centre should be in the business of providing more practical forms of help (e.g. literacy and numeracy classes), and that something should be done to increase their participation in the running and organization of the Centre. The absence of an interesting, 'useful' and 'relevant' programme of groupwork activities is regretted – for different reasons – by both staff and clients.

The current work of Centre 81 is directed at providing help and encouraging client self-determination. In the face of various difficulties, officers have largely reorientated their day-to-day contact with clients from structured group activities to personal relations and informal counselling. This falls within the philosophical approach of treating clients as people and not cases. As Nicholas M. Ragg points out:

It is only if everyone recognises the integrity of personal relationships as an overriding duty and responsibility while in the pursuit of his other objectives, that a high quality of personal

existence can be maintained – an existence in which people know
what they have done and experienced; know, therefore, who they
are. To put one's private objectives above this duty and responsibility is to threaten not only others but oneself, for it undermines the
co-operation between people necessary for the existence of society.
(1977, 44–5)

The recognition of personal integrity reflects a healthy
respect for the self-determination necessary to sustain a full
social existence (cf. Watson and Timms, 1978). In the past,
social work and probation practice was founded on the
unwarranted assumption that offenders suffered from some
kind of internal disorder which required 'treatment'. It is now
widely recognized that the vast majority of clients differ from
their peers only insofar as they have been criminalized.
Generally speaking, the probation service has reorientated its
approach to client supervision by placing emphasis on help
rather than treatment. This is increasingly reflected in the
routine work of officers (cf. Willis, chapter 10 below) as well
as in the attack on various psychological or medical theories of
crime and deviance (Bean, 1976, 65–82). In many ways the
day-care context has become the testing ground for the idea of
helping rather than treating clients.
Day Centres could become a credible and effective alternative to custody. For this to happen on a sufficiently wide scale,
a financial investment comparable to that currently being
made in the building of new prisons is needed. Moreover on
the ideological front, a campaign against the continuing use
(and abuse) of prisons is needed, directed towards both
sentencers and the general public. Clearly a much more active
championing of such alternatives is required of the probation
service; but the experience of Centre 81 demonstrates that it is
essential for the service to be much more professional in
working out the aims and purposes of such settings. One
reason why Centre 81 ran into difficulties was because it failed
to conduct any systematic monitoring of clients' problems and
needs. This paper has demonstrated that even a pragmatic

approach to supervision should be based on a well-grounded appreciation of the difficulties facing clients. Furthermore, the Centre 81 team has failed to identify clearly a 'core' group of clients who could make fuller use of the day-care facilities. This failing particularly applies to homeless and unemployed clients: to groups that are particularly vulnerable and who could be better identified if improved monitoring and gatekeeping procedures were put into effect.

The importance of Day Centres for a 'core' group of clients has been emphasized by Fairhead:

The day centre can ... become the nucleus of co-ordinated policies. Backed up by a network of other support facilities offering, for example, accommodation, treatment for drink problems, and sheltered work, they may allow for positive intervention in cases where this is feasible ... Thus, day centres appear to give the Probation and After-care Service a viable basis for containing petty-persistent offenders in the community, one that they can present to the courts as a feasible way of substantially reducing the prison population. (1981a, 50)

6

The Pontypridd Day Training Centre: Diversion from Prison in Action

Maurice Vanstone

Introduction

The Pontypridd Centre was established as part of the Day Training Centre experiment, which emerged as one of the radical innovations of the 1972 Criminal Justice Act. This Act was considerably influenced by the Wootton Report (Advisory Council on the Penal System, 1970) which had examined the feasibility and further development of non-custodial and semi-custodial penalties. A requirement for offenders to attend non-residential centres was not a new idea in the early 1970s, and a Home Office Working Party, in considering the organizational implications of setting up new provisions, concluded that: 'For certain offenders attendance at a Training Centre where intensive probation supervision would be combined with broad based social education was likely to be the most effective method of treatment' (Home Office, 1972, 7).

The Working Party proposed that 'socially inadequate' offenders should attend Day Training Centres as a condition of a probation order. Underlying this proposal was the assumption that repeated offending resulted from an inability to cope with the demands of day-to-day living. Clients were to be involved in an intensive period of training in the Centre which would lead to an amelioration of their problems and, by implication, improve their chances of coping in the community without recourse to offending. That they were in need of such help was not seen to be in question: 'Offenders of this type will probably have characteristics of a poor work record, limited education, broken or difficult family relationships and poor management of money' (Home Office, 1972, 3).

The provisions of the 1972 Criminal Justice Act were consolidated in the Powers of Criminal Courts Act 1973. Section 4 of the Act specified that up to 60 days' attendance could be required of the probationer, under the close supervision of a probation officer.

A Home Office briefing, based on the findings of the Working Party, gave the four directors freedom to pursue their own ideas in the development of the Centres (the other Centres are situated in Liverpool, London and Sheffield). The Pontypridd Centre, which was opened in July 1973, differs from the other three in that its catchment area has rural as well as urban characteristics. The staffing has remained basically the same throughout its history, although sessional staff were not used in the early years. Staffing is comprised of a director, two probation officers, a workshop supervisor, an administrative assistant, two assistant probation officers and a clerical officer. Additionally, a teacher and domestic assistant are employed as sessional workers.

In its first three years the programme undertaken in the Centre had a distinctly practical and individualist basis, but since then there has been greater emphasis placed on group-based methods of working with clients. Currently the programme focuses on three main areas of work. First, emphasis is placed on social skills and personal problem-solving. This involves the use of a wide range of methods, including groupwork, individual counselling, direct teaching, videotaping, role-play, simulations, films, talks, and pencil and paper exercises. Group members are encouraged to share the responsibility for assessment. This involves the setting of objectives, defining tasks and work to be undertaken in relation to those objectives; and built into the programme there is evaluation by clients and staff of its effectiveness. Second, attention is given

to the importance of practical activities. The Centre's four
workshops are used for a number of activities including
woodwork, metalwork, welding, mould-making, glass engraving and dressmaking. The focus is on achievement and on the
realization of skill potential, and the aim is to provide activities
that are useful and enjoyable to clients. Third, an educational
component forms an important part of the programme. This is
managed by a teacher and involved help with literacy, numeracy and 'O' levels. This work is integrated with the social
skills aspect of the programme.

By concentrating on the above areas of work, the Centre
team has moved away from the traditional reliance on one-to-
one casework and has adopted an activity-based, groupwork
model instead. Groupwork requires that clients become
actively involved in evaluating their behaviour and relationships to others. Skills are built up from this, and are
further used to evaluate the programme in order to make it
flexible in response to changing needs and demands. However, relating clients' views to a more explicit evaluation of the
effectiveness of the Centre requires a more structured procedure, and this will be considered later on in this paper.

The overall aims of the Centre are, first, to provide courts
with an effective and practicable alternative to custodial
sentencing, and second, to establish a setting in which clients
can reappraise themselves and their circumstances, and learn
the skills needed to avoid further offending. There are, of
course, additional secondary aims, the most frequently mentioned by staff being 'confidence building via practical and
social skills training', and 'the development of self-awareness'.

Regarding the aim of providing an alternative to custody,
early evidence of success can be found in a study of the
Pontypridd Centre undertaken by Andrew Willis (1979).
Willis examined a representative sample of clients who had
attended the Centre and made profile comparisons with
imprisoned offenders drawn from the national prison population. The Centre sample comprised 81 people, which was

compared with the national population of adult prisoners received into custody in England and Wales in 1976.

Willis compared the two groups, first, on most recent offence, and found that: 'the greatest preponderance of offenders in both groups are in the burglary and theft categories [which when] combined, account for 59.1 per cent of the imprisoned offenders as against 55.5 per cent of the day centre trainees' (Willis, 1979, 13). Second, the Day Centre and national prison samples were similar with respect to the number of previous convictions. Seventy-five per cent of the Centre sample had six or more previous convictions as opposed to 67 per cent of the prison sample. Thirdly, Willis found with regard to both samples that 'approximately a quarter have no prior custodial experience, a slightly greater proportion have one or two institutional sentences, and about half have more' (Willis, 1979, 16).

A content analysis of the 42 social inquiry reports, which were included in the Day Training sample, revealed that the possibility of imprisonment was raised by officers in 79 per cent of cases. Furthermore, during the year from which the sample was drawn (1976), there were 23 cases in which the recommendation for Day Training was not followed, and in 83 per cent of those cases a custodial sentence was the result. Willis concluded:

Hence, the first charge levelled against Day Training (namely that it is being used in a highly selective fashion) is most certainly true, but not in the sense it implies. Far from it being used as yet another alternative to existing non-custodial measures, and reserved for minor or trivial offenders, the weight of evidence suggests the contrary. In all areas of the country the data supports a substantial amount of displacement from custody, with all the data – comparison with imprisoned offenders, content analysis of social enquiry reports and dispositions awarded when day training recommendations are not followed – pointing to the same conclusion. Day training, it appears, operates as a substitute sentence for imprisonment. In this respect it not only lives up to the penal intent but marginally contributes to avoiding a worsening state of prison overcrowding. (Willis, 1979, 18)

The profiles of the people who have attended the Centre since it was established have been consistently similar to those outlined in Willis's paper. In the Centre's 1982 statistical survey, based on 64 clients, 81 per cent were sent to the Centre for burglary or theft, 76 per cent had six or more previous convictions, and 81 per cent had experienced a previous custodial sentence. There is every reason to believe, therefore, that the Centre continues to function as a direct alternative to custody.

Thus it seems reasonable to conclude that the Pontypridd Centre has catered for people for whom the usual non-custodial sentencing options of the court have been exhausted and who have not been deterred from committing fresh offences by custodial sentences. Having said that it must be conceded that many Day Training Centre clients reoffend after completing the programme, as two surveys have shown. First, a Home Office survey (Payne and Lawton, 1977, 23) showed that, between 1973 and 1976, 53 per cent of Day Training clients were reconvicted with a year of completing training. Second, Willis's survey of Pontypridd Day Training Centre showed that 60 per cent of clients reoffended within a year of completion among those attending from January 1976 to June 1977 (1979, 21). Willis has also estimated that Day Training offers a one in three chance of a decrease in seriousness of offending, when clients leave the Centre (Willis, 1979, 22). These figures are comparable with national reconviction rates on offenders receiving a custodial sentence. Reconviction while participating in the programme is less frequent, however. Thus an internal survey conducted in 1984 demonstrated that 76 per cent of the previous year's intake completed the programme without committing a fresh offence or breaching conditions of supervision.

The client group of the Pontypridd Centre is made up of relatively serious offenders, who are less tractable than the majority of probation clients. The sample upon which this paper is based is made up of people who, during the period from 1 January 1980 to 31 March 1982, submitted written evaluative statements on the Day Training Centre. A total of 59 actually produced statements, but this number was reduced to 38 on whom there were full and accurate profile data. Data were analysed by using a punch-card system. The results showed that the average age of men comprising the sample is 26 years, and average age at time of first sentence was 13 years. The average number of previous convictions is 12.8, this indicating an active criminal career over a considerable period. Furthermore, 91 per cent of the sample had an average of four custodial sentences before attending the Centre.

Although this is only a small sample upon which to base conclusions, the majority of clients have substantial criminal records and have exhausted most of the courts' sentencing options. In other words they are in a situation that is broadly typical for Day Centre clients. Regarding their immediate offences, most committed property offences for which, without the availability of Day Training, they could be expected to have received short- to medium-term prison sentences. All were unemployed when their supervision orders with Day Training requirements were made, and almost 40 per cent had been unemployed for 18 months or more. They have generally suffered from a lack of achievement and tend to have a negative view of themselves, which has been persistently reinforced by others. They are, as Priestley et al. put it, 'the people on the receiving end with the problems', who have often received, even from those paid to help, 'a needlessly second class service' (1978, 188).

The clients' view

The 38 clients for whom full data are available were asked to write down, at the end of the programme, what they felt about the programme and what it had done or not done for them.

The research methods used were relatively simple and unstructured, partly because it was decided that seeking information from clients should form a natural part of their attendance at the Centre. Moreover, the research resources available were modest, and it was also considered important to encourage comments from clients that were spontaneous.

The areas in which clients believed they were helped or gained some positive experience can be summarized, as shown in table 6.1. The research findings indicate that unemployment and shortage of money posed the most serious problems for clients but, as this table shows, these areas were seen to be least amenable to solution by the Centre. In the main, people leave the Centre and return to a life dominated by unemployment. The majority subsist on supplementary benefit, and remain extremely vulnerable to further offending. The worsening economic climate in South Wales gives no hope that this situation will change, and even if new forms of work

TABLE 6.1 AREAS OF HELP AS DEFINED BY CLIENTS

Area of help (rank order)	Number of respondents (n=38)	%
Confidence and personal relationships	25	66
Practical skills	15	39
Being occupied	10	26
Avoiding offending	10	26
Literacy/numeracy	8	21
Outlook on life	7	18
General problem-solving and ability to cope	6	16
Reduction of drinking	6	16
Solving money problems	3	8
Finding work	1	3

do emerge there is little chance that Day Centre clients would be in a position to benefit. Thus the Centre has little or no role to play for integrating people into the employment system.

Regarding the benefits of the Centre, the most frequent references made concerned improvements in relationships and confidence. There were also 15 references made to the practical side of the programme, and these were often linked to an increased confidence, for example: 'Through working in the workshop I have been able to work out more ideas and produce things on my own – this made me feel more confident about what I am doing'; 'I like the craft side most of all and I really enjoy the glass engraving'; 'I have enjoyed ... making things for my new home.'

The opportunity of forming new relationships with other clients was regarded as a major advantage of the Day Centre. The following comments were typical: 'I found mixing with people a lot easier than I thought'; 'I have also come to allow myself the privilege of trusting people and have not come to regret it'; 'I think when I leave I'll have more thought for others and I think I'll be more respectable and a happier person because I usually think of myself but I don't any more.' For another it meant 'the chance to make some friends'.

The single problem most often referred to by clients is lack of confidence, but the variety of demands made upon them and the day-to-day life at the Centre appear to improve this. Client statements range from: 'I feel more confident' to the more profound: 'the Centre would have changed my life when I leave because I would have more confidence.' For others it meant: 'I don't think I am such an introvert as I was when I started the course', and 'Another way I've changed is I think I've become much more confident in myself like. When I first came to the DTC I was a lot quieter and shy and thought people were talking and looking at me, now I don't care as much as I used to. I think the DTC has been a great help to me.'

A major concern of Centre staff is to encourage clients to avoid reoffending. Client comments show that many support this aim, ranging from the hopeful: 'I don't think that I will get into any more hassle with the law', to the more reflective: 'I also know that I am the only one who can stop me . . . I don't want to go down and I think I'm getting too old to get into trouble.' Some clients were even more positive in wanting to avoid prison: 'I am myself determined to stay out of prison with or without the Centre.'

Simply attending the Centre and having something to do there is appreciated by some clients: 'The thing I like most about the Centre is that it occupies me through the days', and 'I have found new pastimes (things to do) which occupy my mind' were typical comments made.

Literacy and numeracy difficulties were acknowledged as a problem by eight people, who reckoned that they had made some progress by attending classes at the Centre: 'I have been catching up on my spelling and also on my maths'; and 'I am more educated than when I came here.'

Seven people felt that their views on life had changed. The following comments were typical: 'My whole outlook on life has changed for the better'; and 'I see things a lot different now that the staff have helped me to sort out a few problems.'

Changes in drinking habits were mentioned by six clients, for example: 'I have cut down on my drinking'; 'I no longer go straight to the pub as soon as I cash my giro'; and 'Occasionally I now have a beer or two but I don't drink to the extent that I used to.'

Six people felt that they were better at coping and solving personal problems. For one, 'it has helped me to look at life in a different perspective and helped me to cope with life'; and for another it had helped in 'coping with people much better and speaking out more'. Another client maintained: 'I am starting to be more assertive in things that need to be seen to. It has been a big help to me coming here, it has shown me what to do in difficult situations and how to handle them.'

Whilst the majority of clients were able to say something positive about their time at the Centre, there were criticisms made both of staff and of the methods used. Favourable

comments were generally directed towards practical activities
and only rarely was a direct link made between the formal
social work content and the improvements and progress
referred to above. Unfavourable comments tended to be
directed towards group sessions rather than particular individuals, for example: 'The Centre could be improved by
having less discussions'; 'I don't think the role play social
skills have been any use to me because they have been
conducted in unrealistic surroundings'; and 'The Centre can
be improved by spacing out the meetings because they get
boring.'

Group sessions were not always seen in negative terms. For
one client, 'Being a member of a group is not a new thing for
me but I have quite enjoyed renewing the experience and the
group discussions were great.'

In general, the staff were viewed favourably, perhaps
because clients did not want to make critical personal comments. Typical responses were: 'I like the way the staff try to
encourage everyone'; 'All the people who work here are good';
'Margo and Marge are really good company. They make you
come out of yourself'; and 'It makes you feel good to see so
many genuine people really trying to help you.'

There were, however, implicit criticisms made of staff
methods, such as: 'There are too many meetings. They are too
long and boring . . . we always talk about the same things all
the time'; and 'I think talking in the meeting isn't getting to
the point, about offending and the reasons why. The Centre
hasn't answered my problems but they [the staff] try.'

Staff attitudes and behaviour were the target for some
criticisms: 'at times I have thought that some of the staff are
petty'; and 'Bad points – childish ways in which the staff treat
us.' The contrasting ways in which clients perceive the Centre
and staff methods can be illustrated by the following statements. First:

I would not recommend this place. This place has messed me up. Of
all the institutions I've been in I would not like to come to this place

again if it were not for the threat of prison. There are too many personal discussions and so much distrust. It's very strenuous – you have to make an effort to control your behaviour. I'm up against authority here. I can't stand it. I'm anti-authority. It's not heavy but you still feel it.

And second:

This course has helped me to be consistent, got me out of a rut, gave me the chance to make some friends; helped me to see my problems in a new light so I am better able to deal with them. It's been a completely new experience in my life for the better, helped me to stay on the right side of the law, brightened up my outlook on life. I've not been so depressed since I started. I've been able to cope with drink, not get into trouble with it. I feel more optimistic about life and overall I'm glad I was given the opportunity to be here, p.s. everybody's been just great.

The staff view

According to the staff, the main purposes of the Centre are to enhance clients' self-confidence and self-awareness, and to help them to develop practical skills. However, clients tend to relate changes in the former areas more directly to the practical work and to the day-to-day life of the Centre, and do not see these as being related to officers' particular social work methods. It is difficult for staff fully to understand the client point of view. Self-examination and problem analysis, whether in groups or individual counselling sessions, are both difficult and not always appropriate for or wanted by clients. The staff team has had, therefore, to confront the question of how much choice about the type of methods should be left to clients. This is difficult for social workers and is not an issue normally encountered in conventional casework. A basic respect for people dictates that it is important, however. Additionally, staff morale is likely to be low if clients are consistently unenthusiastic about their methods, since this is likely to make the programme less effective by impairing staff motivation.

Consequently, Centre staff have had to accept the need to re-evaluate their perceptions of social work skills. Second, staff have learned to accept that the provision of an environment in which clients can develop and sustain social relationships is in itself a legitimate form of social work. Finally, the need to provide clients with real choices and to seek their views, and to take clients' criticisms seriously, have been recognized by staff.

In an attempt to further the development of probation officer/client relationships, changes have been introduced in the work of the Centre. The current twelve-week programme has two distinct phases, in which the content varies according to decisions that clients make. The issue of client choice within the context of probation supervision has been discussed by Malcolm Bryant et al. (1978). The authors proposed that offenders placed on probation should be required to fulfil a primary contract between themselves and the court. On making this contract, the clients then negotiate their own subsidiary contracts with their probation officers. Bryant and his colleagues suggest that: 'on each visit ... [the client] should be asked by the receptionist if he would like to see a probation officer and could opt into the other resources of the agency if he chose but would not be required to do so under the primary contract already referred to' (1978, 111). The general issue raised by Bryant et al. is that clients should be seen more as 'consumers' able to exercise the power of choice, thus enabling them to be provided with services that are useful and relevant to them.

In order to help clients make informed choices about the programme of the Centre, the following procedure is currently used. During the first four weeks, people are expected to participate in a series of eight group sessions. The focus of these sessions is on the individual's offending history and on personal strengths and weaknesses. Discussion and exercises are used in order to encourage full self-examination. At the end of these sessions, group members are given the programme checklist to complete, which contains all the options available within the Centre. From this point group members decide for themselves the content of their personal programmes. This is then discussed and written down at a meeting with their probation officers. Centre staff then use the checklist to organize and plan both the practical and social work aspects of the remaining part of the programme. With a recent intake, sessions were set up based on the areas of confidence, feelings, drink, leisure, drugs, family, money, accommodation, rights, and job search. On the practical side, basic electrics, plumbing, car maintenance and home decorating were taught. The range of subjects confirms that the demands made by clients are extensive, and the programme thereby becomes broader than if based only on what the staff think is appropriate.

Conclusion

It has been shown in this paper that the staff of the Pontypridd Centre are concerned about the effectiveness of social work intervention, seeing this as being related to the clients' point of view, which has to be elicited and used in planning activities. It was also because of the desire to elicit the clients' point of view more fully that the research upon which this paper is based was undertaken. In considering the complex question of effectiveness, it has to be acknowledged that the views expressed by those at the receiving end are not in themselves a sufficient criterion of success. Experience at the Centre has led staff to the opinion, however, that such views should be given greater weight than has generally been accorded by social workers and their managers.

Any claims about the effectiveness of the programme for changing criminal behaviour must be treated with caution. Furthermore, such claims involve making some risky assumptions about the reasons for offending and about the appropriateness of social work action for inducing a reduction in offending. Working in the Centre has led staff to the view that if social workers can successfully extricate themselves from the strait jacket of the treatment model and its incumbent theoretical assumptions, then they will become more effective as social workers. By enabling clients to make informed choices, they are better able to give help pertaining to those problems which are most important to clients. Within the Day Centre setting, it has been possible to help people improve, among other things, their levels of literacy, their confidence and their ability to form social relationships. The main issue is not whether solutions to such problems can be put into effect, but the extent to which they can be achieved more consistently. The flexible application and use of various methods that are stimulating and relevant to clients form central features of the staff's approach. Effectiveness in these terms is realizable, although a reorientation in social workers' perceptions of their role is required. A client-centred approach, based on a variety of objectives, should not be considered of lesser importance than the attempt to realize such specific goals as the reduction of offending.

Judging from the client comments in this paper, it would seem to be both realistic and more honest to pitch social work objectives at the level of providing tangible forms of help for clients. Staff at the Pontypridd Centre believe they have put into practice the method suggested by Bottoms and McWilliams, who argue that 'the case worker offers unconditional help with client defined tasks – this offer having certain definite boundaries' (1979, 170).

The ability to put into practice Bottoms' and McWilliams' 'paradigm of help' depends to a great degree on social workers' willingness to listen and to respond positively to the views and needs of clients. The clients' views presented in this paper illustrate that such an approach can constitute an effective form of social work in a Day Training Centre context. The further development of the type of social work intervention undertaken at Pontypridd could result, moreover, in a more humane and relevant response to the problem posed to society by the more serious offender.

7

The Failure of Supported Work: The Bulldog Programme

John Pointing

Introduction

The Bulldog scheme was established in October 1975 by the Inner London Probation Service (ILPS) as a rehabilitation programme for chronically unemployed probation clients. Its overall objective was 'to turn some of the most troublesome clients . . . towards a lawful, self-sufficient, wage-earning way of life, by employing them for a transitional period in a supported work situation' (Bulldog Report, 1976, ii).

The rhetoric of rehabilitation pervades the early literature about Bulldog.[1] In part this was necessary to satisfy its financial sponsors – the Home Office – but it was also because Bulldog was explicitly modelled on American methods of social work intervention. The development work on Bulldog was undertaken by the Vera Institute of Justice, which in the early 1970s had set up the Wildcat Service Corporation in New York. Wildcat was a non-profit making organization designed to provide 'jobs for the chronically unemployed among former heroin addicts, criminal offenders, and other "unemployable" groups' (Wildcat Report, 1978, 1).

Wildcat's claims that a deviant and problematic client group could be turned into economically productive citizens was attractive to policy makers in the Home Office and probation service. Although the ILPS did not have a large number of heroin addicts on its books, it was felt that the supported-work

106

concept pioneered by Wildcat would be equally applicable to a hard core of intransigent recidivists in their late teens and early twenties. However, Wildcat's clientele bore no comparison with Bulldog's, with the exception that both schemes recruited people having interrupted or non-existent work histories. The Bulldog clients are discussed in detail in the course of this paper; Wildcat's clients were described as follows, in 1978:

60 per cent were black, 30 per cent were Hispanic, and 10 per cent were white. On the average, they came to the program at age 31, with a police record of eight arrests and four convictions. Typically a sample member had become addicted to heroin at age 19, had been addicted 11 years, and had been enrolled in a drug treatment program for one year. About 80 per cent ... were referred to Wildcat from methadone maintenance programs. (Wildcat Report, 1978, 2)

It is important to bear in mind the rehabilitative objects of Bulldog as defined when it was set up, since they persisted for a long time in influencing programme managers' decisions and provided a rationale for the continuation of the scheme.[2] The basic assumption underpinning rehabilitation in this context was that the provision of an environment bearing a close approximation to 'normal' work would enable offenders to obtain a footing in the 'world of work'. This, in turn, would enable clients to live 'normally' in society, without recourse to criminal activities, the underlying assumption being that there exists a causal relationship between unemployment and offending.

The above definition of the situation was expressed in Bulldog's First Annual Report in the following terms:

The programme is about habits – breaking old habits and supporting the formation of new ones ... The Company's aims [viz. Bulldog's] have been to break [old] ... habits and to help them [the clients] into the habits of attending regularly at a worksite, taking home regular wages, paying taxes, putting in a full week's work, and applying themselves to tasks demanded by work supervisors. The work habit could help them play a productive part in the economy over a long term. The continuing lack of it threatens, in a few years time, to leave them in a cycle of unemployability, offending and imprisonment – a permanent drain on the resources of the penal system and of the supplementary benefits programme. (Bulldog, 1976, ii)

There is no evidence to support the view that Bulldog has achieved the rehabilitative results that were expected by its initiators. In the comparatively undepressed local economy of the late 1970s a few people worked after leaving, but the severity of the 1980s recession has meant that an improvement in employment relations is unachievable except for a handful of people. This paper demonstrates that these were the more skilled and capable, and they mostly had relatively good work records before starting with Bulldog.

Despite its inability to put into effect its primary objective, Bulldog continued for a long period with Home Office grants (almost £500,000 in 1981) and funding from the ILPS. Moreover, it still functions, albeit in a much more modest way than from 1975 to 1984. Part of the reason for this is because Bulldog demonstrates the willingness of a social work agency to do something about what is commonly seen to be an appalling problem for offenders: a cycle of deprivation, unemployment, offending and imprisonment. It is thus plausible that schemes such as Bulldog afford a kind of psychological relief to people who either have to work with offenders having problems which are not perceived as amenable to more traditional forms of social work action, or to managers of social work organizations who feel the need to respond to pressures coming from front-line workers. Neither should it be overlooked that employment as scheme managers in Bulldog offered an attractive route for long-term career development to field probation officers.

A further benefit of running such a prestigious project has probably been that the ILPS gained project development skills which have facilitated the setting-up of other new programmes in different fields. However, this kind of gain is a spin-off and the main purpose of this paper is to consider those benefits obtained by probation clients having poor employment records and substantial custodial experience for whom the scheme was intended. It is demonstrated here that although Bulldog's clients gained little in terms of improved employment prospects, there were tangible gains nevertheless. For reasonable numbers Bulldog afforded a break from rhythmic containment in prison establishments, and for a substantial proportion the setting provided security and the chance of developing new social relationships. More prosaically, Bulldog successfully provided a form of temporary work for people with interrupted work histories and for some who had no previous employment. This work consisted mainly of low-grade painting and decorating, though gardening and metal work were provided for relatively small numbers. The work was organized along lines bearing a similarity to conventional forms: jobs were closely supervised, clients could be fired and were paid wages near to market levels. The disciplinary focus of the scheme was derived from employment relations, and clients' probation orders were kept distinct from employment in Bulldog so no one was breached and brought back to court merely for being fired.

The Bulldog research programme

Bulldog was a highly innovatory project of the 1970s, particularly since it was situated in an otherwise traditional bureaucracy: the ILPS. The need to legitimize its position in that bureaucracy, the objective in the 1970s of the Home Office to extend the Bulldog model to other areas of the country, and the reliance on American methods of social work intervention, have meant that research has played an important role in Bulldog's development.

The research upon which this paper is based was undertaken between the spring of 1980 and the autumn of 1982. Its purpose was to evaluate the effectiveness of the scheme from the clients' point of view. A sample of 84 clients, comprising the entire intake between March and October 1980, was interviewed three months after starting work. A second follow-up interview was conducted with as many as could be contacted around a year after leaving the scheme. This sample comprised 51 clients. The two sets of interviews were carried out between June 1980 and July 1982, and timing was varied to take into account differences in starting and leaving dates.

The 84 clients in the first interview sample were mainly male (90 per cent); 50 per cent were black and the remaining 50 per cent were white. Their ages ranged as follows, from the time of first interview: 62 per cent were aged between 17 and 21, 32 per cent between 21 and 25, and 6 per cent were aged over 25. Thirty-six per cent of the sample (n=84) worked for three months or less in the scheme, the remainder for between three and 18 months. There was a slight tendency for older and black clients to stay longer.

Both sets of interviews consisted of open-ended discussions with subjects about work, unemployment, offending, and more specifically about Bulldog. The majority of interviews lasted from around 1 to 3½ hours. Subjects' employment and offending careers were reconstructed in the course of interviews, and these, together with the scheme's role in facilitating changes in people's work situations, formed the main lines of discussion. Changes over time constituted the main basis for comparison, with the three-year period before going to Bulldog being compared to the 12 months after leaving.

From the analysis of interview data it was found that in most cases individuals' employment situations became worse over time. In quantitative terms, the proportion of clients working under 30 per cent of time available increased from 53 per cent (pre-Bulldog) to 71 per cent (post-Bulldog). Over the same time spans, those working between 30 per cent and 70 per cent decreased from 41 per cent to 14 per cent, and the proportion working over 70 per cent of time available increased from 6 per cent to 16 per cent. These figures take into account time lost to custody, which is defined as time spent unemployed. Thus other than for a small group of eight clients, there was a marked decline in the time people spent working between pre– and post–Bulldog periods. This was partly due to the generally deteriorating unemployment situation during the period when this research was carried out, but it also resulted from the scheme's inability to foster and develop new skills and to provide adequate training, so that clients could have obtained jobs on leaving.

This paper is based on the recognition that Bulldog has failed to achieve its primary objective of effecting a transition from unemployability to post-programme employment. This problem of Bulldog's failure is compounded because the client group sought for recruitment to the programme remained elusive. Bulldog's formal criteria stipulated that on entering the programme clients must 'have a poor (or non-existent) work record in the previous two years and during that period must have held no job longer than three months' (Bulldog, 1980, Appendix ii). Only 54 per cent of the first interview sample fall within this criterion, the remainder having had too good a work record.

However, the sample was comprised of people with substantial criminal records. During the three-year period before going to Bulldog, 18 per cent of the first interview sample were convicted for theft; 47 per cent for burglary, robbery, or TDA; and 12 per cent for offences of violence. Moreover, during the same timescale, 56 per cent of the first interview sample spent periods totalling 10 per cent or more in a custodial institution. The corresponding figure for the post-Bulldog period (one year) was 39 per cent.

In summary, we can see that Bulldog achieved little in terms of improving clients' positions in society. In terms of the amount, stability and level of post-programme employment the results are largely negative (cf. Pointing, 1982, chapter 2). This earlier research also showed that only marginal changes occurred over time in the rate of reconviction and seriousness of new offences. The role of Bulldog in effecting slight improvements in these areas was described as follows:

Although differences in the periods of comparison can be allowed for, this being an obvious reason for observed attenuation, we still cannot ascribe causal significance to Bulldog as a reason for this attenuation. Bulldog may or may not help in reducing the incidence of offending, and a small number of subjects did argue in both interviews that they were helped by Bulldog in this respect. Even with these clients, Bulldog only acted as *a* source of help and no client attributed prime importance to Bulldog over other factors. (Pointing, 1982, 84)

The results of this earlier work did show, however, that reoffending while participating in the programme was comparatively rare.

The rest of this paper will be concerned first with examining Bulldog as an agent of help and change from the point of view of clients in the research sample. Discussion will concentrate on intrinsic benefits, namely those specific to the programme and to the period of working in Bulldog. Second, some of the implications raised by Bulldog's failure as a supported-work scheme will be considered in the conclusion.

Client evaluations of Bulldog

The fieldwork forming the basis of this paper is composed of client 'accounts' which constitute a rich and complex source of data. These data have not been used to describe and analyse clients' views about the world in general, though this is an important task for research in social work settings. Rather these accounts have been used as a basis for evaluating the effectiveness of Bulldog as a social work programme. The justification for giving primacy to client accounts partly depends on the assumption, made throughout the course of this study, that clients were the subjects whom the scheme was intended to benefit. It also arose because it was felt that the interests of subjects could be enhanced by giving credibility to their accounts.

It is possible that the primacy given in this research to client accounts will be found objectionable. The label 'client' enshrines a definition of inadequacy on the recipient; and some members of the 'caring professions' may find discomfiting research which gives credibility and validity to the client point of view. Taylor's (1972, 23) critique of this type of assumption, though applied with respect to social scientists, is more generally apposite. Taylor castigates social scientists who claim that deviants' accounts lack plausibility in relation to non-deviants' accounts, since they assume that *only* deviants: 'inhabit a behavioural world in which motives and the accounts offered of them lack correspondence. Social scientists ... [thereby] accord purely epiphenomenal status to the deviants' verbalized reasons, believing that inner drives, instincts, conditioned reflexes, internalized goals, constitute necessary and sufficient motives for action.'

The assumption underlying this research is that validity can be accorded to client accounts to the same extent as can be given to non-deviant accounts. Research subjects, in the main, were found to be conversationally willing and competent in the course of research interviews; and the researcher tried to see subjects as experts, but not soothsayers, regarding the questions under discussion, and thus to treat subjects as knowing providers of information.

The validity which is accorded to these accounts is also consistent with the view that offenders have rational objectives. This paper demonstrates that sample members possessed rational expectations about what they could gain from the scheme. On the whole, they perceived Bulldog as a job or as a similar experience to working in an ordinary job; and they further assumed that their prospects of working in the future would be enhanced by participating in the scheme. Generally they found after leaving Bulldog that their chances of working again were slim, and this often led to disappointment or

resentment. Many clients, particularly by the time of second
interview, recognized that the vicious circle they were caught
in with regard to unemployment had not been broken by
Bulldog.

Client evaluations and perceptions are presented in this
section in the form of summarized categories, which are
abstracted from a much finer level of detail contained in
interview schedules. Client objectives in going to Bulldog,
assessments of the work and training content of the scheme,
and perceptions of help, form the main lines of discussion. In
this section, materials are drawn from both sets of interviews:
the first set (n=84), undertaken when most clients were still
working at Bulldog, and the second set (n=51), consisting of
those who could be contacted 12 months after leaving.

Table 7.1 reveals that clients' reasons for going to Bulldog
often involved more than one factor. The desire to obtain
work and learn skills predominate, and factors 1 and 2
combined were cited by 61 subjects. Most of these thought

TABLE 7.1   CLIENTS' REASONS FOR GOING TO BULLDOG:
FIRST INTERVIEWS

Factors cited (rank order)	Number mentioning factors (n=84)
1 To get work experience/job, or as alternative to unemployment	48
2 To get qualifications/learn skills	26
3 To please probation officer/family	18
4 To change lifestyle	8
5 To give up crime/alleviate police attention	7
6 To impress court because of pending appearance	7
Others	5

that going to Bulldog would constitute a means whereby more permanent forms of work could be secured in the future. The 23 remaining clients were made up mainly of those wanting to please their probation officers (more frequently than family), those wanting to change their lifestyles by becoming 'workers', and of those wanting to give up regular crime or alleviate unwelcome police attention. Seven out of these 23 subjects cited 'strategic' reasons for going, pertaining to pending court cases. These clients, on the initiative of their probation officers, believed that being in work would enable them to be 'let off' with respect to pending court appearances.

Table 7.2 consists of a summary of the differences between client preconceptions and experiences of Bulldog. Overall, the table shows that 66 out of 84 subjects (79%) felt that their actual experience differed in some way from what they thought the programme would be like before going. The table also suggests that work and training formed the essential

TABLE 7.2 AREAS OF DIFFERENCE BETWEEN PRECONCEPTIONS OF BULLDOG AND ACTUAL EXPERIENCE (N=66): FIRST INTERVIEWS

Area of difference (rank order)	Turned out more than expected: Column 1	Turned out less than expected: Column 2	Not mentioned Column 3
1 Enjoyable work	26	23	17
2 Training	14	26	26
3 Like a real job	9	18	39
4 Strict regime	3	17	46
5 Like probation	4	14	48
6 Friendly people	18	0	48
7 Hard work	1	13	52
Others = 10			

factors for clients in evaluating their experience of the programme, and that the ways in which clients perceived Bulldog
fit fairly well with their reasons for going. The results shown
in Column 2 of table 7.2 indicate that many people were
critical about the type of work done in Bulldog, and about the
amount and level of training given.

Table 7.3 demonstrates that Bulldog was perceived by most
interviewees either as a job or as a comparable experience to
working in an ordinary job. The responses also reveal complexity in that differences between Bulldog and other work
places are seen in positive as well as negative ways. Although
low proportions are involved, more than twice as many
thought Bulldog a better as opposed to a worse place to work
compared to others. But for a substantial minority, Bulldog
was run badly and, in comparison to others, was a worse firm
to work for. It would seem, then, that at the time of first
interviews Bulldog was seen by one group of clients as a fairly
congenial work environment. For another group, it was seen

TABLE 7.3 COMPARISONS BETWEEN BULLDOG AS A 'FIRM'
AND OTHER FIRMS: FIRST INTERVIEWS

Client descriptions (rank order)	Number of clients mentioning each description (n=84)
1 Bulldog different as a firm from others	55
2 Better firm to work for than others	37
3 Run worse than others	22
4 Worse firm to work for than others	18
5 Generally similar to other firms	15
6 Run better than other firms	8
7 Run equally well as other firms	5
8 Equally good firm to work for as others	4
Other descriptions	8

as insufficiently demanding and poorly organized, and many of these had already left by the time of interview.

Before reconsidering these issues with respect to follow-up interviews – which were undertaken about a year after sample members had left Bulldog – some broader issues associated with the scheme's role in effecting change and help will be discussed. The material is therefore still based on first interview data.

Table 7.4 isolates changes pertaining to work and future employment and quite starkly suggests that most people did not see the scheme as an agency of change. Only 45 per cent of the sample reckoned that they were receiving (or had received) benefits directly related to the experience of work which might further their prospects of future employment. Again there is an underlying complexity to these responses. Many amongst those feeling they had benefited seemed both highly optimistic and committed to the ideal of becoming a worker. On the other hand, a majority of those who saw no change were either fatalistic about their employment prospects, or had worked

TABLE 7.4 PERCEPTIONS OF BULLDOG AS AN AGENCY OF CHANGE REGARDING FUTURE EMPLOYMENT: FIRST INTERVIEWS

Client perceptions (rank order)	Number of clients (n=84)
1 No change	45
2 Change in desire/feelings/skill	14
3 Change in skill only	8
4 Change in feelings only	6
5 Change in feelings and skill	6
6 Change in feelings and desire	4
Don't know	1
Total	84

little in the past and had no intention of working in the future. Some of those in the majority group, however, had very good work records and saw no reason to worry about finding new jobs in the future. Overall, these results suggest that people assessed their chances of working in the future in terms of what had happened before going to Bulldog rather than while working for Bulldog. It would appear, moreover, that working in the scheme was seen as an interlude both by those seeing it in mainly positive terms as well as by those viewing it negatively.

Table 7.5 provides a further source of information, based on whether sample members saw Bulldog as a provider of tangible forms of help. Thirty-one people said they had had no help and 53 maintained that they were receiving (or had received) 'some' or 'considerable' help from the scheme. Considering the former group of 31, 24 of these had also said they did not see Bulldog as an agency of change. Thus almost one-third (29 per cent) of the sample had decided, within three months of starting, that they were not receiving any form of help from Bulldog and would not be in a better position to secure employment after leaving.

The types of help mentioned by the 53 subjects indicating 'some' or 'considerable' help are summarized in table 7.6. The

TABLE 7.5   PERCEPTIONS OF BULLDOG AS AN AGENCY OF
HELP: FIRST INTERVIEWS

Client perceptions of Bulldog (in general)	Number of clients (n=84)
1 Made things worse	3
2 No help	28
3 Some help	36
4 Considerable help	17
Total	84

findings suggest that clients perceive help in various ways which pertain mainly to the work carried out, but also to perceptions of self, relations with others, and to the incidence of reoffending. Most of those seeing the scheme as providing 'considerable' help also said that Bulldog had served to change their feelings about work, their desire to work regularly in the future, and had helped them to learn new skills (cf. table 7.4).

The results considered so far suggest that within three months of starting to work in Bulldog, around two-thirds of the sample felt that some benefits had been gained as a consequence of this experience. Such an assessment to a large extent depends on whether gains associated with work have been made but also, if to a lesser extent, on how the social environment induced by the scheme is perceived.

The importance of organizing the scheme as an effective and real work environment is also borne out by the responses of the more critical clients, who did not perceive Bulldog as having provided them with help. Thus 24 out of 31 of these critical respondents thought that Bulldog could have helped if

TABLE 7.6   SOURCES OF HELP MENTIONED BY CLIENTS (OUT OF 'SOME'/'CONSIDERABLE HELP' RESPONSES): FIRST INTERVIEWS

Source of help (rank order)	Number of clients (n=53)
1 Associated with work tasks/activities	41
2 Associated with work routine	30
3 Pertaining to perception of themselves/ self-confidence	22
4 Associated with relationships with family, friends	14
5 Helped to reduce criminal activity	12
Others	7

120   JOHN POINTING

certain operational changes were made. The changes cited are given in table 7.7, and these demonstrate very clearly the importance attached to work factors.

Table 7.8 consists of an attempt to provide a typology of client attitudes to Bulldog and is based on a qualitative assessment of materials drawn from a variety of sources. This has been done because although a majority reckoned that they were receiving tangible benefits from the scheme at the time of first interviews, a substantial proportion of interviewees were nevertheless critical about the way the programme was delivered. This table shows that although 25 clients were considered to have identified themselves positively with Bulldog and its objectives, almost as many (21) denied the legitimacy of the way it was organized. Such people were often highly articulate in criticizing 'tokenism' in the scheme, and sometimes attributed hypocrisy to its objectives or to staff members. The attribution of 'tokenism' was made, first, by those who saw Bulldog as an attempt 'to keep them off the streets',

TABLE 7.7   WAYS BULLDOG COULD HELP (OUT OF 'NO HELP' RESPONSES): FIRST INTERVIEWS

Ways it could have helped (rank order)	Number of clients (n=24)
1 If work more 'real'/pleasant/varied	16
2 If better management/better foremen/more incentives to work hard	14
3 If taught formal skills/gave a trade certificate	11
4 If paid better money	6
5 If placed you in a job on leaving	5
6 If quality of workmates better	3
7 If hired for longer period	1
Others	5

i.e. as a form of social control. It was also levelled by those critical about the poor quality of jobs available, the low standards of skills and training, and the low wages paid. A few argued that Bulldog's primary purpose was to provide safe, cushy and well-paid jobs for probation officers and their ilk. This table does not show, however, that many individuals were either indifferent to the scheme or particularly hostile to the people running it.

The remaining part of this section will deal with the results of second interviews. We would expect significant variation in accounts between first and second interviews, although not so much because follow-up interviews are likely to be more truthful or accurate due to the fact that no one was still working for Bulldog when these were carried out. Differences are more plausibly explained by changes in immediate employment situations. Thus all respondents were working, or had until recently worked, when first interviews were undertaken, albeit in Bulldog. In contrast, in the year between leaving Bulldog and taking part in follow-up interviews, 49

TABLE 7.8 OVERALL ATTITUDES TO BULLDOG: FIRST INTERVIEWS

Overall attitudes (rank order)	Number manifesting attitude (n=84)
1 Client identifies with schemes	25
2 Client denies legitimacy of way scheme organized	21
3 Client indifferent to scheme	11
4 Client hostile to staff running scheme	9
5 Client accepts necessity of way scheme organized	3
Impossible to classify	15
Total	84

per cent of the sample (n=51) had not worked at all, 35 per cent had worked a little, and only 16 per cent had been working regularly (Pointing, 1982, 24).

During the follow-up interviews, discussion again took place with subjects over whether working in Bulldog had helped in finding and keeping jobs since leaving. With those who had not worked at all since that time, discussion was based on subjects' assessments of their chances of working in the future. Out of the 51 individuals who could be contacted for a follow-up interview, 11 said that Bulldog had helped them to get jobs or improved their chances, five said it had helped slightly, and the remaining 35 felt it had made no difference. In the course of these interviews, time was spent discussing whether Bulldog had amounted to a 'real' job. For 19 out of these 51 subjects it had been 'real', partly because it led to something afterwards. For the majority, it was seen as a 'scheme', 'con', or 'pretend job': this suggested disappointment with Bulldog's incapacity to effect change. Although some subjects expressed bitterness about Bulldog, or felt betrayed by those probation officers who had referred them or by Bulldog's work supervisors and managers, most people also blamed themselves for not working. Only rarely did subjects see causes in simple terms; the majority interpreted their own situations as resulting from personal failures, Bulldog's lack of provision of suitable work and skills training, and a generally worsening unemployment situation.

In table 7.9 a summary is given based on the types of help provided by Bulldog, as seen from the retrospective viewpoint of second interviews. This table is composed from the responses of the 11 clients for whom Bulldog served as a source of help in regard to post-programme employment, and from those of an additional 26 clients for whom the scheme was seen as having been useful or helpful in other ways. It is interesting to note that despite the general discontent with Bulldog as a scheme designed to promote employment, a majority of clients could still say positive things about it after a year of leaving.

TABLE 7.9   AREAS OF 'HELP' AS SEEN BY CLIENTS IN RETROSPECT: SECOND INTERVIEWS

Area of help (rank order)	Number mentioning each area (n=37)
1 Learning skills/getting some form of training	25
2 Providing situational stability	20
3 Providing means to learn work routine	19
4 Improving perception of self/ self-confidence	12
5 Providing basis for career aspirations	11
6 Provision of job/alternative to unemployment	7
7 Enabled subject to reduce offending	3
Others	7

Overall, the results in table 7.9 are consistent with earlier findings, and areas of help directly associated with work retain their priority. Moreover, many responses allude to environmental and social factors, specifically the provision of situational stability and enhancement of perceptions of self. People thus attributed to Bulldog benefits of a purely social work nature, similar to those that may be explicitly delivered in a Day Centre or Day Training Centre.

These results show that Bulldog clients' longer-term perceptions of the scheme tended to be orientated to wider benefits than its formal objective to provide a transitionary setting for transporting people to the 'world of work'. This does not mean, though, that Bulldog actually provided long-term gains. During second interviews, subjects were asked to recall the time spent working for Bulldog, and then, retrospectively, to decide about its benefits during that time and not at the time of interview. Such cognitive processes are of course highly selective. Most individuals would have based their responses in the light of recent experience, which for many, amongst the majority who had not worked at all or only a little since leaving the scheme, was perceived as a worse period of their lives than the interlude filled by Bulldog. It seems reasonable to conclude, then, that although the benefits of situational stability or improvements in self-confidence may not have had longer-term implications for clients, nonetheless such benefits were important to people at the time of working in Bulldog, and thus were selectively retained in their memories along with their negative assessments.

This interpretation of the findings is consistent with the results shown in table 7.10, which highlight areas of failure elicited during second interviews. These areas of failure are exclusively concerned with work factors. In comparison with the results obtained during first interviews, the table demon-

TABLE 7.10   REASONS FOR BULLDOG'S FAILURE TO 'HELP' AS SEEN BY CLIENTS IN RETROSPECT: SECOND INTERVIEWS

Area of failure to help (rank order)	Number mentioning each area (n=51)
1 No proper skills/training given	21
2 Did not enable subject to find job afterwards	17
3 Scheme not run properly	16
4 Not 'real' work	11
5 General unemployment situation makes scheme non-viable	8
6 Bulldog staff did not fix up a job on leaving	6
7 Subject not a suitable referral	4
8 Bulldog did not provide a skill certificate	1
Others	15

strates that subjects were becoming increasingly critical over time. This is not surprising since by the time follow-up interviews were conducted, most subjects perceived their chances of future employment as minimal. Not only does this suggest an underlying rationality in clients' responses, but it also explains what at first glance appears as a paradox: that a majority of subjects were critical of the employment and work aspects of the scheme but, additionally, viewed other aspects germane to the setting favourably. Had Bulldog operated formally as a Day Centre, client responses may have been more favourable. This seems debatable, however, since the situational stability provided by the scheme may well have been the product of routines based on work, and explicit forms of social work intervention could have been resisted by this client group.

Criticism about the way the Bulldog programme was run formed a substantial part of the follow-up interviews, and this has to be put into context. Bulldog was set up to solve the problem of chronic unemployment amongst 'troublesome' probation clients; many subjects went to work in the scheme because of the belief that this would help them obtain reasonable jobs in the future; and many hold conventional ideas about the importance of work and evaluated the scheme in terms of those ideas. Disappointment and even resentment were experienced by many subjects after discovering that Bulldog did little to change their prospects of future employment; feelings that were exacerbated by doubts as to their personal capabilities and awareness of a generally deteriorating unemployment situation. This goes a long way towards explaining why subjects' views about the scheme became increasingly negative between research interviews.

Nevertheless, it may be concluded from the evidence presented in this paper that Bulldog was a badly-run initiative, and that it should have adapted to changing economic circumstances rather than persisting for so long in the pursuit of unrealistic formal objectives. Finally, this paper casts doubt as to the general feasibility and appropriateness of delivering social work intervention in the guise of controls derived from supported work.

Conclusion

It has been shown in this paper that as a supported-work scheme the Bulldog programme was largely a failure. To a degree this was the result of pitching objectives too high, notably that of changing the employment situation of clients from pre-programme unemployability to post-programme regular engagement in the 'world of work'. This study has also highlighted some disquieting features that are not satisfactorily answered by this point. Central among these are the scheme's failure to equip people with the skills and knowledge to find subsequent jobs, poor supervision and management, and the incapacity to develop a sufficient range of work for its clients to do.

Bulldog's demise has not been a clear-cut case of programme failure, however. The underpinning of the scheme by an employer/employee relationship seem to have allowed 'naturalistic' social relations to develop, contrasting favourably with the sometimes strained and artificial atmosphere to be found in Day Centres, for example. Some clients experienced the opportunity to engage in significant social relationships, or found that the scheme provided a stable episode in their lives. This research has also shown that work constituted an important need for subjects: a client group deemed unemployable by probation officers, but on the whole possessing the work 'ethic'. This calls into question the need for rehabilitation in cognate schemes: careful organization geared closely to the likely post-programme situation seems more necessary than concentrating on individual motivation and the inculcation of new habits.

This research also raises doubts regarding the viability of supported-work schemes in periods of economic recession. This arises not only because Bulldog was seriously undermined by the general shortage of jobs, but because any such scheme either needs to employ people permanently or give them the means to work independently on leaving. The former option implies a stable work force while demand for spaces continuously increases, because other employment routes are blocked in current economic conditions. Similarly, independent working requires a long-term programme, is subject to demand pressures, and suffers from closure of alternative routes. Both options are likely to be extremely expensive to run mainly because of low throughput.

Nevertheless, some pointers to the future of supported work can gleaned from the provision, for the right client group, of the means to work independently. The research on which this paper is based (Pointing, 1982) showed that some subjects were resourceful in finding their own alternatives to conventional jobs. From this research it was concluded that working casually to supplement state benefits was a strategy undertaken, often as a conscious alternative to theft and burglary, as a way of obtaining a reasonable living. Teaching people a variety of ways of making money, particularly those based on casual and informal forms of work, would be a tangible gain for the type of clients Bulldog was set up for, and possibly for a wider range than this. Toleration of this principle of supplementation of state benefits of course depends on wider social factors: most importantly, acceptance and recognition in social security legislation would be needed.

Another approach to encourage independent working could be pursued through community development. Environmental and housing improvement in areas of particular deprivation (such as those occupied by Bulldog clients) could be undertaken by community-based organizations and organized by them rather than public bureaucracies. Such a model is more common in the US, and experience there suggests that new political structures as well as substantial economic resources are necessary (Shearer, 1984). Nevertheless, recent research in Britain on alternative ways of managing and improving local authority housing stock gives some hope for future changes

(Anderson et al., 1985). In association with community development, skills training organized on the basis of a secure
and varied source of work has an exciting potential. Evidently
initiatives of the scale and imagination needed to put such
community programmes into effect are not on the political
agenda at present. The involvement of hitherto deprived
groups in the community, including probation clients, could
amount to such groups securing real gains from which further
benefits might ensue.

A final general issue raised by this study is that supported
work, organized to encourage independent working, could be
explicitly based on educational lines. Probation clients could
be taught skills orientated to future employment, but the
forms this employment would take could be geared to coop-
erative and self-employed models. It was clear in the course of
this research that subjects wanted to learn skills and make
products for their own sake, but that many did not want to
work in conventional work settings and some did not want to
work regularly. People often wanted to work on their
terms rather than someone else's; work tended to be seen in
complex terms rather than simply as a way of obtaining a
living. There seems little unconventional in these attitudes,
and being able to work independently if irregularly would
constitute a tangible gain for most of the subjects of this study.

The possibilities outlined above are offered as pointers to
challenge the present impasse regarding the employment
prospects of probation clients and similarly deprived groups.
The human and financial resources required to effect any
significant change are formidable, and the prospects of such
resources being made available by the present government
seem negligible. Such options could, of course, be pursued
with the savings released from the planned closure of prisons,
which makes much logical as well as practical sense. However,
the building-up of resources other than the financial presents
far more difficult problems. In particular, we need to confront
the 'conservative consensus' paralysing decision makers'
minds in the government and the civil service, and also in

social work organizations. We thus need to challenge those responsible for continuing to pursue inept penal policy, and maintain pressure by exposing their failures to confront the problem of what could and should be done *with* offenders, as distinct from what is being done *to* offenders.

NOTES

1 Summaries of early research findings, including those of Home Office researchers, can be found in Bulldog Annual Reports, namely those for the first year (1976), second year (1977), and fourth year (1980), all published by ILPAS.

2 The Bulldog programme was drastically cut back during 1984, and continues in residual form with much more modest aspirations. Since this time, only a metal workshop and a small works department remain from the earlier programme. This paper was written before this cut-back, and the arguments presented here apply specifically to 1980–2 and more generally to 1975–84 with respect to programme objectives. The years from 1978 to 1982 witnessed the programme at its peak in terms of size. During this time, around 25 supervisors and managers were employed at any one time and there were approximately 100 places available for probation clients.

8

Options for Problem Drinkers

Helen Bethune

Introduction

In one sense, a paper on Alcoholics Recovery Project (ARP) Shopfronts has no place in this book, in that the relationship between the Shopfronts and their clients is entirely voluntary and unconnected with any form of statutory order. In another sense it is entirely appropriate, in that if drink is not taken, drink-related offences do not take place. Drink-related offences, therefore, rate more than a passing reference in any book concerning alternatives to custody.

In April 1983 I interviewed a random sample of 24 visitors to ARP Shopfronts. Of the 24, 21 had criminal records varying between two offences to 'near enough a hundred'. One respondent, a woman, could only give me her name and age. 'I'm not sober', she said, and indicated that she could or would talk no more. Two said they had no criminal records.

What a drink-related offence is can be variously interpreted. For the law itself, and for the purposes of official statistics, there are four broad categories: drunkenness offences (with various additives), drink and driving offences, under-age drinking and, peripherally, licensing infringements. But for the alcoholic offender, the categories may be seen to be somewhat different. Here are four respondents answering questions about their records:

130

'I'd wake up in a cell, knowing nothing and ask "what have I done this time?"' said Judy (21). 'I can't deny it because I can't remember ... I've been on loads and loads of charges ... criminal damage, assault, threatening words and behaviour – don't know where they got that one about the words, drunk and disorderly ... all over London I've paid fines.' (She'd been in two women's prisons.)

'Always drunk when I got into trouble', said Bill (43). 'I'd never dream of going into a shop and shoplifting unless I was drunk. It's as though someone else takes over.' (Bill had about six different offences on his record, among others the time he had physically assaulted a security man when he was trying to do some shoplifting.) 'Tried to strangle him. I had money on me at the time, that's the funny thing.'

Steve (36) has had five offences: two assaults, one police assault and two for breaking and entering 'for money for drink'.

Joe (42): 'Can't remember how many times I been in prison. 20, 30, 40 times? A night, 6 months, a year ... mostly for being drunk.'

Drink-related offences would therefore be classified by the alcoholic as: (1) offences committed in blackout; (2) offences, not necessarily drunkenness, committed after drink has been taken; (3) offences committed in pursuit of alcohol or money for it; and (4) straightforward 'drunk' offences.

Of the 21 Shopfront respondents who admitted to having records, 12 said they had been told they had a drink problem/alcoholism by magistrates, probation officers, psychiatrists, judges or doctors, some of them on numerous occasions. Some people had been admonished, some sent to detoxification units, two put on Section and two had been sent to treatment units. 'A judge said to me "You're trying to kill yourself"' said Dave (27). But he still carried on for some time, drinking and committing further offences 'related to drink or to get the drink'.

ARP does not only maintain Shopfronts. Shopfronts are a part of the organization which aims to provide a complete service for homeless alcoholics, and to this end it also runs a number of dry houses. During the early part of 1982, I spent a week in each of six hostels, in the course of which research I also interviewed 34 residents individually. In the sample, only two residents appeared to have been involved in offences which were not drink-related. One was a con-man, whose speciality was donning the classic gear of the clergyman or RAF officer, and whose work therefore demanded sobriety. From his history, it appears that he did not become compulsively addicted to ethyl alcohol until fairly recently, after a long and relatively successful career in his chosen profession. The second man did not want to disclose his offence. All the rest of the respondents whose criminal careers were discussed appeared to have committed their offences either as a consequence of, or in pursuit of, alcohol.

Drawing the line between drinking and alcoholism

For the observer, the law-enforcer or the carer, the distinction may be difficult to make between the 'villains' who merely have a pint or two to get some 'dutch courage' to perform whatever they intend to perform, and the alcoholics who may behave apparently similarly, but who are compelled to their actions by the overwhelming authority of the condition of alcoholism from which they suffer. As Kessell and Walton put it years ago, 'Alcohol addicts are unable *spontaneously* to give up drinking' (1965, 16). On the other hand, the American Medical Association states categorically, 'Alcoholics are treatable patients' (1977, 7).

This, the oldest of humankind's afflictions, is still surrounded with great mystery and still subject to enormous and often emotional debate. To some extent this emotional content reflects two aspects of the response to alcoholism which also bedevil the law-enforcers and carers who come into professional contact with alcoholics. On the one hand there are the 'normal' people, who can safely and cheerfully enjoy a sherry or a few pints and get happily (or unhappily) tight now and then without worse consequences than a mild hangover. For these people, it is difficult not to feel gut-level distaste for the lack of self-control so blatantly manifested by the alcohol addict. To accept the concept of alcoholism as an illness is often difficult for alcoholics themselves. It can be even harder for some of those whose business it is to sit in judgement or proffer advice and help.

However, because alcoholism *is* an illness, which knows no frontiers, no barriers of age, sex, class or profession, it can and does also afflict some of the law-enforcers and carers themselves. Magistrates, probation officers and social workers (to name but a few) are not guaranteed immunity against contracting alcoholism. One of the respondents in the Shopfront sample had indeed been a care assistant in more than one local authority. This man had gone all the way down to the park bench, but what of the person who is just beginning to suspect that their drinking is getting a little out of hand? The 'normal', temperate drinker really cannot understand the nature of the problem. The 'endangered' drinker may have one of several responses, not all of which may be helpful. He or she may impose unnecessarily punitive sentences or conditions which reflect self-disapproval as much as anything else, or may studiously ignore the relationship between drink and trouble in an offender's history.

Fred, a Shopfront attender aged 45, had had years of drink-related crimes. He had been in prison countless times, he said. When I encountered him in a Shopfront, he was on a suspended sentence. He is an engaging and articulate man, and for the previous 13 years he had been great friends with a senior probation officer. According to Fred, never once in all those misspent years had the officer suggested there might be a connection between his criminal offences and his drinking. It would not be unrealistic to question whether the officer himself were 'endangered'.

On the other hand, there are many professionals who do understand the nature of alcoholism and its protean manifestations, and make appropriate responses to alcoholics. Judy's probation officer was aware that most of her actions had occurred in blackout. He collected her entire record and confronted her with it. She was appalled. She had no idea that she had committed so many offences and misdemeanours. Striking while her defences were down, he suggested – not ordered – that she might find help if she wanted it and gave her directions for getting to the Shopfront. His factual confrontation and common-sense approach were perfectly timed: she asked for help at a Shopfront.

One of the most important functions of ARP Shopfronts is that a breakthrough is reached when a person first enters the door. A person appearing in a Shopfront implicitly is conceding the possibility, if not the actuality, of alcoholism. It may be noted that the younger people are at the point of defining their alcoholism, the greater the hope for recovery. What they then decide to do about it, and how much of the offered help will be accepted, will depend on many variables. As Edwards points out: 'one of the certain lessons of close experience is in fact that this condition is recoverable, and there are pathways off skid row, however difficult to find' (1982, 62).

What is a Shopfront?

If you were not looking out for it, you could easily pass by an ARP Shopfront without noticing it. Intentionally, the Shopfronts keep a very low profile. All three are in London, in places where public drunks are most visible and therefore most socially offensive. The New Cross Shopfront is in a small run of shops on a busy main junction. In Kennington, it is less a Shopfront, more a part of a church hall. The Kings Cross Shopfront is down the road from the mainline station. Kings Cross and New Cross simply display in neat lettering the words 'A.R.P. SHOPFRONT' and give the times of opening: two hours every morning, Monday to Friday.

Ten minutes after opening time, there will probably be

between 12 and 25 people sitting round with paper cups of tea or coffee in a thick fug of roll-up tobacco smoke. Most of them will be men but there may be a woman or two. They are there because they have one thing in common: they are alcoholics, though their last drink may be anything from ten minutes to ten months away. For that reason their physical appearance will vary from the filthily disreputable to the spruce and neat. By the time these people have got to an ARP Shopfront, they will also probably share a number of other social characteristics. Family life will have collapsed. Regular employment is a thing of the past. They will mostly be homeless, having spent the previous night in a reception centre, night shelter, hostel, squat or police cell, or simply sleeping rough. Almost to a man (or woman) they will be past, present or potential clients of the probation or prison service, and past, present or potential clients in a detoxification facility, a psychiatric or other hospital. These latter facts neatly illustrate the familiar problem which alcoholism poses for its victims, and which alcoholics in turn deliver up to society at large: are they bad, mad or sick?

Shopfront history

Shopfronts were pioneered in this country in 1970 by ARP: 'to assist homeless alcoholics into a treatment/rehabilitation system so removing men from punishment within the penal system ... Homeless alcoholics have been defined as hard to reach by traditional social work methods' (Archard and Cook, 1974, 1). Shopfronts provided a new way to reach those parts of the deviant population which other agencies could not reach. Siting them in areas frequented by drinking schools was considered to be of the first importance. The habitat of the vagrant alcoholic is the street, and Shopfronts were strategically opened at street level.

It was also important to maintain an informal, unstructured, non-bureaucratic setting. Social work time, expertise

and professional advice were on offer, but there would be no
handouts. Limited hours of opening were an integral part of
the scheme. Shopfronts were designed to capture the intransigent, chronic alcoholic and set his or her feet on the path to
rehabilitation, perhaps initially by way of hospital treatment,
thereafter through an alcoholic hostel, typically one of the dry
houses which ARP runs.

Both the Home Office (1971) and the DHSS endorsed this
imaginative venture, and by 1974 results from a pilot survey
provided reasonable evidence that a sample of Shopfront users
had significantly higher rates of admission to hospitals and to
alcoholic hostels – 'believed to be the major rehabilitation
facility' – and markedly less contact with the courts than two
control groups with similar records of drunkenness convictions (Archard and Cook, 1974). Today the goals of the
Shopfronts remain as before, although two of the three have
been resited. Only St Anselm's survives *in situ* from 1970. The
aim is still primarily to get the alcoholic to do something about
his or her drinking problem, preferably by means of regular
attendance with a view to entering an ARP dry house for
treatment/rehabilitation. Most of the staff also see themselves
as providing a vital contact point, counselling service and
support system for homeless alcoholics.

Uses of Shopfronts

For the clients, a Shopfront clearly serves many purposes. At
one level it is a place to come in off the street, to spend a
couple of hours without hassle; it is a place to read the *Sun* or
the *Mirror* (or the social worker's *Guardian*); it offers tea,
coffee, a chance to clean your shoes or to have a shave. At
another level, it ensures a private conversation with one of the
two social workers, an opportunity to iron out problems with
the DHSS (there are *always* problems with the DHSS), to get
referred to a detoxification, medical, housing or other facility.
A Shopfront is not a social club, but neither is it an impersonal

office. While one social worker is in a small back room talking a problem over privately or making a telephone call, another will be sitting with the regular attenders and visitors, making them welcome and trying to win them over to considering a change of lifestyle, or simply to listen. For one hour an Attenders' Group is held in another room for those hoping to be accepted into an ARP hostel.

Hard data about who uses Shopfronts and for what purposes are difficult to come by for three reasons.

1 The nature of Shopfronts is, as was indicated, casual and unstructured. If they are doing the job properly, Shopfronts offer a low-key and unthreatening welcome to anybody who wants to drop in. There is no compulsion for clients even to disclose their identity if they do not want to. There is good reason for this as I regrettably have occasion to report. At one time I was doing a spot check on the operation of the ARP central filing system, and to this end I inquired of every person present one morning in a Shopfront just his name and whether he had ever been a resident in an ARP hostel. All went well until I came towards a man who visibly trembled as I approached him. I smiled, explained my name and purpose. 'I'm just here for some tea', he managed to stammer: and with that he put down his cup and fled. The incident also illustrates vividly how easy it is for a researcher to contaminate the setting.

2 Even given a willingness to cooperate, the mental condition of the still-drinking or newly-dry alcoholic has to be borne in mind. Not only will a Shopfront respondent have probably incurred a degree of (perhaps temporary) brain damage, he or she will also, if still using alcohol, be suffering from some impairment of both short- and long-term memory (Kessell and Walton, 1965, 35–9).

3 The researcher must be alive to aspects of the full-blown alcoholic personality, much documented in the literature and amply supported by evidence from recovered alcoho-

lics. These include lying, shame, guilt, grandiosity, resentment and very low self-esteem. Any or all of these can
make for very unreliable responses even to quite simple
and straightforward questions in a Shopfront.

Who uses Shopfronts?

For the above reasons, the following analysis of Shopfront
users should be read with caution. Where possible I have
taken note of social workers' weekly record sheets and sat
around talking with the clients. I have used my ears and eyes.
Shopfront clients appear to fall into six categories as outlined
below.

1 The familiars. These are people who have already been in
ARP houses and may still be in one. According to the
records, just under 25 per cent of Shopfront users fall into
this category. They are self-selecting. The majority of
these people will be hoping to be accepted once again into
the Project.
2 New referrals who are seriously thinking of doing something about their drink/housing problems, and who are
willing to undertake the assessment programme, which
currently takes approximately four to six weeks, depending partly on the social worker's assessment of the client's
potential for rehabilitation and partly on the bed situation
in the hostels. The numbers vary from week to week. In
each Shopfront there could be from one to six people in
this class.
3 New referrals who are just 'testing the water': perhaps
one or two a week.
4 A small number, directed there by another local facility,
'illegitimately' using the Shopfront as a Day Centre.
(This appears to apply only to one Shopfront.)
5 A small number who want to persuade another agency
(notably probation officers) that they are cooperating.

'Might get three months knocked off my probation', confided one informant.

6 Finally, there are the people who use the Shopfronts for a range of services which may be for them otherwise quite difficult or even impossible to obtain. A Shopfront offers an exceptionally attractive blend of uninstitutionalized but professional services which can provide distinct advantages for those in the know.

Records kept by the primary social worker in the (relatively) new Kings Cross Shopfront of telephone calls and personal contacts, during the three-month period 5 March to 4 June 1982, illustrate this point. The range of calls was very varied, many of them made on behalf of clients, though a proportion were concerned with notifying other facilities of the existence of the Shopfront.

Apart from in-house calls, there were 117 calls to or from clients, 61 calls about accommodation, 82 to hospitals or detoxification facilities, 45 to probation officers, 35 to prisons, 22 to social serives, 25 to other dry houses and 67 miscellaneous calls which included GPs, Area Health Authorities, family, friends, courts, local authorities and other agencies. This does not include a vast number of calls made on behalf of clients or by clients themselves to the DHSS.

What this information shows is that the connections and specialist expertise of the social workers are being used by people who might otherwise have little or no access to medical, housing or welfare facilities. Shopfront workers pride themselves on following an 'open door' policy with clients. Consequently they open doors for a special group of the underprivileged homeless population.

The ages of the clientele

Accepted wisdom has it that the average Skid Row alcoholic is in his or her late forties. The research on the ARP appears to support this contention if one is concerned only with the mean age. However, those people who are seen to be requesting help from the Project, either through the hostels or in the Shopfronts, appear to have a very wide age distribution, with very few over 60.

The mean age of the 34 hostel residents interviewed was 45.8 years. However, they were distributed by age across a span from 30 to 61 years, with only a very slight clustering in the mid to late forties (see table 8.1). The interviews were partly structured, partly unstructured. I was concerned, *inter alia*, to discover when each person recognized that drink was a problem, and if possible at what age each respondent realized they had begun 'serious' drinking.

Of these 34, nine admitted to serious drinking by the age of 15 or less. Five of these were aged between 30 and 40 at time of interview. The remaining 25 had either graduated over the years of heavy drinking into alcoholism or had perceived a sudden change in their drinking habits at or around a time of

TABLE 8.1　AGE DISTRIBUTION OF HOSTEL RESIDENTS

Hostel residents		
Age	*No.*	*Percentage*
30	1	2.9
31–5	5	14.7
36–40	4	11.8
41–5	7	20.6
46–50	7	20.6
51–5	3	8.8
56–60	6	17.6
61	1	2.9
Totals	34	100%

crisis, notably when a spouse had thrown them out. It is interesting that of the seven hostel residents aged 39 or less, five admitted to having started serious drinking or drug-taking at a very early age: one at 15, two at 14 and two at 13.

A distinction can be noted between when a person actually knew they had a drink problem and when, with hindsight, and with no 'drink taken', they were able to perceive how drink had affected their lives. The memory improves wonderfully the further away from a drink an alcoholic gets, and it seems likely that many respondents were unable to remember how early they had started serious drinking in their lives.

The random sample of 24 Shopfront users produced the data about ages shown in table 8.2. It should be noted that every effort was made to interview not only people who noticeably made themselves available but also people who were slightly more hesitant about being questioned or talked

TABLE 8.2 AGE DISTRIBUTION OF SHOP-
FRONT VISITORS

Shopfront visitors

Age	No.	Percentage
21–5	2	8.3
26–30	2	8.3
31–5	—	—
36–40	5	20.8
41–5	8	33.3
46–50	3	12.5
51–5	1	4.2
56–60	2	8.3
61	1	4.2
Totals	24	100%

to. Nonetheless the importance of not disturbing the setting (referred to earlier) was considered vital and therefore no attempt was made to structure either the sample or the interview in any formal way. The figures should still provide a reasonable indication of the composition of the Shopfront population.

Of the 24 respondents, eight 'knew' they were drinking alcoholically before they were 30 years old. The two oldest men could not put a date to their recognition of the problem, one answering 'I realized when I began missing Mondays at work', but both knew it was a very long time ago.

The denial process

In all the debate and discussion which bedevils the subject, at least one issue appears to receive general agreement. This is the existence of the denial process.

By *denial* is meant a defence against reality which is based on a refusal to admit the existence of that reality: it is oneself rather than others who have to be deceived. In pure form the mechanism is pictured as operating at a subconscious level, with denial thus differentiated from a conscious untruth which is aimed at the deception of other people. Often, though, the patient's initial difficulty in facing up to the threat of his drinking is a manifestation both of denial in the classic sense and of prevarication. (Edwards, 1982, 307)

Charlie (27) described the process as he had experienced it: 'There are three stages', he said. 'Other people knew it first. Then I knew it but wouldn't admit it. Then I admitted it to myself – and started doing something about it.'

As is painfully clear from the mortality rates (however inexact they may be), the 'something' which the self-acknowledged alcoholic may do about it is precisely nothing. 'I am an alcoholic therefore I must drink' is a not unfamiliar response. It is the response of despair. Many, however, do try to stop drinking, and some happily manage to stay away from alcohol for varying periods of time: even for the rest of their lives, though rarely without some help.

It is also generally agreed that recovery from the condition of alcoholism can be effected only through the alcoholic's personal and private decision to stop drinking.

Before that decision is even a possibility, there will be the lies. Not only will there be lies about the amount drunk, but there will be denial that there is a problem about drinking at all. As Edwards points out, the lying may be in part subconscious, in part deliberate. One respondent said in a Shopfront, 'I thought if I admitted I was an alcoholic, I'd be locked up.' Breaking through these lies, laying bare stark reality, is essential if recovery is to occur. Ultimately the onus is on the alcoholic him- or herself, but a nudge – especially an official nudge – can do no harm. 'Anyone with my troubles would drink like me' is most helpfully answered with the response: 'Anyone who drinks like you is bound to have your troubles.' But unless hope is offered and help suggested, the alcoholic may retreat into a defeatism which admits of no recovery. Suicide is an only too common consequence of alcoholism.

The decision to do something positive about stopping drinking (which an alcoholic will probably make on many occasions during a lifetime), appears to depend on many variables and be person-specific. For one alcoholic it may be the first appearance before a magistrate, for another it is a fleeting awareness that life has become intolerable *with or without* booze. Alcoholics Anonymous calls this moment a 'rock bottom'. At this moment all denial is swept away and the alcoholic faces the reality of his or her relationship with alcohol.

It has been suggested that no alcoholic stops drinking voluntarily: in other words that pressures of the consequences of drinking are gradually or suddenly perceived to be worse than the thought of living without drink. It is interesting to note that neither the hostel nor the Shopfront samples held any people aged over 61. One might speculate that those few

who have survived death or a locked ward beyond that age can
see little hope in an alternative future.

What certainly is clear from the research is that many
alcoholics are afflicted with the condition from a quite early
age, and official recognition of this can do no harm. Jim, a
jockey aged 38, had started drinking at 15. He made up for not
being able to drink during the week by having monumental
binges at week-ends. At 23 he recognized he had a drink
problem. 'Getting ready to go to mass on a Sunday morning I
started to shake all of a sudden. Couldn't do me tie up. My
landlady said the trouble was drink.' He saw a doctor. 'He said
I was on the way to being an alcoholic. I said I was one
already. I laid off it a good while – two years. But I began
again.' It was not until many convictions later, at 36, when he
had appeared 14 times before the same magistrate, that it was
officially put to him that he do something about his drinking.

The doctor's tentative reference to 'being on the way to
becoming an alcoholic' is unfortunately not untypical of some
of the myths surrounding alcoholism, particularly in respect of
age. Sources in Alcoholics Anonymous report that the age of
members is visibly declining. Grey heads no longer predominate in meetings. Many a fresh-faced youth and maiden can be
seen at any of the 1,730 meetings throughout Great Britain
held each week. The fact that one-sixth of a random sample of
Shopfront visitors are under 30 bears out the concern of the
Minister of State at the Home Office (in a speech, 11
November 1980):

The figures of offences for drunkenness tell us only part of the story
about under age drinking . . . drinking is starting at a much younger
age than in the past. Of those in the youngest age group interviewed
(18–25) the average age at which they began to drink was 16
compared with an age of 20 reported by the older age groups. This
was linked to a considerable increase in the proportion of people who
said that before they were 18 they had had a drink in a public house
(from about 13% in the past to 70% in 1978). (Raison, 1980)

There are simply no cut-and-dried answers to many issues concerned with alcoholism. But certainly breaking down some of the denial process can do nothing but good. Ignoring the relationship between drinking and its consequences only prolongs the alcoholics' self-deception that they are 'getting away with it'. Recovering alcoholics frequently refer to the fact that the only people they fooled were themselves. But it is not always appreciated by professionals and people in authority how much their words and actions may help, as in the case of Peter.

Peter (32) was in one of the hostels, working at his recovery. He had not drunk at all until he was 24. 'I was up in court for theft, and the question came up, "Why?". I answered, "Money for drink". I got a conditional discharge – and went out and drank straightaway. Was back next day before the same magistrate who asked me if I had a drink problem. I said, "I don't know". The probation officer told me I had a drinking problem.' This was now his fourth attempt to get sober. He may make it, he may not. The point is that he has now identified himself as a person with alcoholism, and that at least gives him options. Only *he* can stop the elbow-bending which will, if he continues to drink, inexorably lead to more prison terms, hospital treatments, and usually a very squalid death.

9

'Oh God, It's Going to be Awful': Clients' and Officers' Perceptions of Adventure Activities

Patricia Maitland

I dreaded it at first . . . I knew drink would be a problem. I thought without the drink – oh, God, it's going to be awful. To be honest, I thought I would be trapped on the side of a mountain with a group of people I couldn't get away from. I knew I would not be able to get up and walk away which I usually do. But when we were there I didn't want to do that. When we started to put the tents up there was no time for thoughts like that. As I said, I would go back tomorrow, it was the best weekend of my life.

Introduction

This statement made by a client of the Inner London Probation Service (ILPS) illustrates the feelings of many clients who were interviewed in the course of this study. First of all there is anxiety, not primarily about the activity itself, but about being amongst strangers, followed by enjoyment of the event. Then, in many cases, there is enthusiasm for more participation. The quotation has been used to begin this paper because although adventure activities have been regarded as legitimate forms of social work for many years, they are still seen in some quarters as 'soft options' or 'treats' for bad boys. It is hoped that the present paper will go some way to dispel this myth. Second, it is hoped that the motives behind probation officers' use of this type of social work intervention will be clarified. Finally, the paper explores clients' views of the activities undertaken.

The research on which this paper is based took place in 1980. It looked at all the clients who had participated in adventure activities with ILPS during 1979. The demographic details of a total of 76 client were examined; and interviews were conducted with 36 clients and 39 officers. In addition, sessions of participant observation were undertaken, in which the researcher accompanied several groups on their weekends and participated in the activities.

Working with clients through activities appeals to some probation officers more than to others. Officers who regularly become involved with such activities tend to be relatively young, often having similar experience based on previous employment (e.g. the Navy), and most have continued to pursue sports or outdoor hobbies as leisure activities. Much of their enthusiasm for this type of work springs from personal conviction about the value of physical challenge and achievement rather than being based on a particular social work theory. They see activities as an effective way of working with clients, who either require additional help or a different approach to individual counselling.

This perspective is supported by Thorpe's (1978) description of the purposes of IT: 'The "treatment" of intermediate treatment may very simply be seen as the provision of a non-delinquent career, rather than some esoteric psychotherapeutic experience which would in all probability be beyond the scope and skills of the average social worker' (70).

The provision of choice and new opportunities were objectives cited by many of the probation officers interviewed in this research, who saw their clients' lives as often lacking legitimate outlets for energy and excitement. The use of clients' leisure was often described as being over-reliant on money-consuming, mechanical sources of entertainment, which were seen to be without challenge and unable to provide a lasting source of satisfaction.

The aims of the activities were not, however, seen simply as a way of providing deprived clients with the fun they lacked in life, but were regarded as a means by which they could learn something new and change in some way. Officers claimed not to be influenced by any social work theory in having such objectives, but the underlying philosophy seems similar to that expounded by Priestley et al. (1978): 'We do not assume that people are sick or in need of treatment. We assume instead that most people would like to learn how to cope with some of the situations in their lives in ways that are more effective or more congenial to themselves and others' (11).

A typical weekend away

In 1976 ILPS set up the adventure activities programme. The intention was to provide the opportunity for officers and clients to leave London and undertake ventures such as rock climbing, camping, canoeing, and even parachute jumping. Each party usually left London on Friday evening in a hired minibus. The destination was either a camp-site or self-catering cottage. The next two days would be spent divided between the activity itself and cooking, tidying the accom-modation, walks, talks, and most likely a visit to a pub. All the tasks would be shared between group members. The officers would at every chance try to encourage the clients to take the initiative and be responsible for some aspect of the weekend, the cooking, tent pitching, etc., and only intervene when difficulties arose. Where the activity required a skill at least one staff member with the relevant experience would lead the group.

Who took part in adventure activities?

The demographic details of the 76 clients showed that the majority of the clients were white, single men under the age of 23. Few women took part (only 6.5 per cent of the sample were female compared with 18 per cent of all clients supervised by ILPS), and there were few clients from ethnic minorities (14 per cent).

Basic demographic data appear at one level to support a conventional picture of clients undertaking adventure activities, namely that activities are being provided principally for fit young men who are thought to respond better to an 'action' type of social work rather than to traditional casework.

The average number of previous convictions for the sample was six. Three out of five clients had been involved in offences of dishonesty of some description. The most frequently mentioned were theft, burglary, deception and TDA. Next in number came clients who had been involved in crimes of both dishonesty and violence, ranging from minor assaults to manslaughter.

It is noteworthy that 23 clients (30 per cent) were involved with violent offences, a higher proportion than for the ILPS clientele as a whole. Most violent offences took place while the client was carrying out an act of dishonesty. Only four clients had been convicted for violence alone: their offences ranging from sexual assault to hitting out when provoked by children. Nearly all the clients had had some form of steady employment in recent years. This may reflect a bias amongst probation officers towards 'deserving' clients, although only one probation officer actually stated that the trip was a 'reward' for her client. However, work also prevented clients from going on weekends where Friday evening or Saturday working was necessary.

Half of the clients in the sample were on probation at the time of the activity. The majority of the rest were on after-care, generally from Borstal, and a handful were voluntary clients. Two-thirds had experience of custody, in most cases Borstal, with only a few having been to prison, which is as would be expected given the relatively young average age of the sample (21 years).

Sixteen clients were known to be educationally subnormal and six were illiterate. Eight clients had a drink problem and four were addicted to hard drugs.

An unexpected finding, however, was that 25 per cent of the sample had histories of mental illness: a finding which challenges assumptions that clients on adventure activities are all tough and boisterous. In the majority of cases, the illness went back to childhood: mainly schizophrenia, psychosis or simply 'personality disorders' were diagnosed in case files. In addition, three clients with mental health problems were intellectually subnormal. There was a tendency for clients who had been or were mentally ill to be older than the rest of the sample (average age 30). Another important point is that a relatively high proportion of this group of clients, half in fact, had been involved in offences of violence. Three of the four clients who had been convicted solely for violence against the person had histories of mental illness. These individuals' level of participation in the activities was similar to that of clients without such problems, and their enjoyment appeared to equal, if not surpass, that of the other clients. Despite this client group's ability to cope with the physical aspects of the activities, considerable skill was often required on the part of the organizing probation officers to dissipate tension arising within the group as a whole. Such tension, and at time flashpoints, resulted from the other clients' limited tolerance of the sometimes odd behaviour of those with mental illnesses.

The selection of clients

There were two ways in which clients were invited to take part in an activity. First, they could be encouraged as individuals to join a party that their probation officer had either initiated or knew was being organized by other officers. These clients went individually, rarely knowing the other group members. The second way was through attendance at 'clubs' organized by probation officers. At the time of the study, six such clubs were flourishing in the ILPS. They provided a social setting for officers and clients to meet informally, and anyone wishing to join could do so. Most clubs organized weekends away as well as other outings as part of their programme. Thus some clients were selected because their probation officer identified their having specific needs, whereas others were included with no particular aim in mind, the weekend away often being a development from mainstream club activities.

The officers' objectives

The most frequently cited reason given by the officers in this study for encouraging clients to take part in an activity was to 'improve social skills'. This description included learning to cooperate with others and enabling clients to gain more confidence in personal relationships. Next came the hope of broadening the clients' horizons and wishing them simply to have fun. For some, it was hoped that a spin-off would be an improvement or development of the client/officer relationship.

The replies of officers who felt that their clients needed to improve their social skills indicated that clients were frequently seen to be not in control of their behaviour, or could see little point in trying to control it. This tallies with the findings that a high proportion of clients had histories of violent offences. Officers felt that many clients were either unaware of the effect their behaviour had on others, or simply accepted the fact that they were disliked. The relationships between adventure weekends and improving social skills were described by officers in the following terms:

A low tolerance level has always been his problem. He could do a lot of damage to someone if he lost his temper. The weekends would, I thought, teach him to control himself.

It was a socialising thing. He talks so much he wears people down, and so loses all his friends. It was intended to help him get over that.

He needed to be in a controlled setting where he had to make himself acceptable to others.

He needed to be in a situation on a long term basis, to be in a group that would not tolerate bad behaviour for long. It is easy to be nice in an office once a week, but much harder to live out the consequences of your own behaviour over a two-day period.

It was an opportunity to prove to himself that he could be liked by others.

A few officers stated that their clients had particular difficulties in relating to women, and some of these had been convicted for serious assaults on women. One officer referred his client: 'To let him see that you can communicate with women without hitting them'. In the officers' view, clients' lack of success with relationships was due not simply to not knowing how to form relationships but lacking the confidence to try. If the clients' self-confidence could be raised, argued several officers, then problems in forming relationships would be lessened:

He has a very poor self-image, a small lad, gets bullied by younger brothers. He is always bossed around by people. I hoped the weekend would give him confidence to stand up for himself.

He may not appear to lack self-confidence, but [is] very shy, needed to be boosted up.

To show him he is a person of worth, that others will accept him.

Another frequently mentioned goal of some probation officers was a widening of their clients' horizons. In the view of many officers, their clients' lives were narrow and often routine:

That lad had never been in a place that does not have lamp-posts!

The weekend enabled him to see the countryside for the first time in his life – to see animals. He has little conception of what exists elsewhere.

I encouraged him to go on the weekend because he needed to do something other than the mechanical type of entertainment that he always finds for himself, such as drinking, TV, gambling, etc.

Other officers, more ambitiously, hoped their clients would be introduced to pastimes that could divert them from their criminal activities: 'I referred him to let him see that stealing cars is not all there is to life.'

Officers' evaluation of the activities

When evaluating the benefits of weekends, many officers claimed that the activities helped their clients to gain confidence and to form better relationships. Some argued that their clients simply looked happier after going on a weekend:

After his first trip, he came into the office with a big grin. He held his head up, walked better, and told me all about it. Very different from the sullen sulky lad who used to have nothing to say.

He talks more at home now, and has stopped hitting his mum.

He now has a different way of communication; people are possible to know. Before, he felt he would just be ignored (which he often was) unless he made an inappropriate approach (generally assault).

Several officers argued that clients talked more willingly and with more confidence after going on weekends, and some stated that they also found supervision sessions more pleasurable. Even if the officers did not take part, having the weekend to discuss added a new dimension to conversation and provided a pleasant alternative to such topics as job hunting, family, or payments of fines.

In some cases officers felt their clients had made substantial gains from weekends, which extended beyond the officer/ client relationship:

He is more self-assured, he has lost his restlessness. He no longer runs off home on a whim, but he will discuss the fact that he wants to go.

He no longer needs to offend to get attention.

He appeared to be much more self-confident, more independent. He has moved out of a hostel and is living in his own accommodation.

Probation officers' claims about improvements in levels of social skills and self-confidence are supported by the number of more confident clients who subsequently developed new interests. The following quotes illustrate the type of gains made:

He now regularly attends a folk club and even goes to evening classes for music. Also plays football for his firm's team. He has moved out of the probation world a lot.

He has been supported from every angle, but now his order is finished. He has made contact with a local settlement near here, and is going to work with handicapped people.

He began to expand his relationships; he became very friendly with the people who ran a cafe nearby and began doing work for them.

For some probation officers the adventure activity was seen as providing an opportunity to get to know their clients in an informal setting. This was felt to be particularly valuable since the majority of meetings with clients occur in places of 'authority', i.e. probation offices, Borstals, detention centres, courts. The benefits of improved communication have, moreover, a spin-off for subsequent meetings in formal settings. As one officer argued: 'During the weekend I got to know him better. Seeing him in Borstal he was lethargic and uncommunicative and we had a very poor chance of communication ... It helped our relationship very much, I would never have got to know him otherwise.' Another officer stressed the importance of obtaining better quality information in informal settings:

Drink is a great problem for many of our clients, but there is no point gearing the weekend away from any possibility of drinking. If the clients get drunk and abusive, perhaps it is as well that we are there with them to see just what goes on; instead of getting secondhand stories of drunkenness from wives or girl friends, as we would in an office type situation.

Clients' evaluation of the activities

It could be argued that such an intangible concept as 'improved social relationships' is immeasurable when evaluating the benefits of weekends, and could just as easily be put down to wishful thinking by probation officers. However, the testimony of several clients also claiming improvements in this area supports the officers' observations. The following are typical examples of clients' comments:

I have always had difficulty getting on with people I don't know well, but I am much better at it now. That's really coming to the club and going on the weekends. Also, I got a job in a shop, which has helped.

Years ago I used to be a very funny character. I know that's hard to believe now. When I came out of prison years ago, I was always on drugs, over-drinking. I was very aggressive, couldn't talk to anyone properly. I tried to commit suicide several times. Then I started coming to the club and away at weekends and everything sort of turned around. I wasn't drinking so heavily, slowed down on drugs. I had a few binges though, with a couple of bottles of whisky inside me I would perform on the table-tennis table, but not now. I wouldn't behave like that now. It has given me a different life altogether.

Although no client actually stated that his 'horizons had been broadened' by going on a weekend, several talked with excitement of what they had seen or done:

I have done things on these weekends that I would never have done on my own, canoeing, rock climbing. I never thought I could do things like that.

The best bit of the whole trip was the view of the cliffs from the sea. It was wonderful. I have never seen anything like it in my life. Some of the weekends we have had, I will never forget them, never. I think about them now back in London.

The claim of officers that weekends improved communication was also supported by several clients. One argued: 'You can relate to them [probation officers] more, in a different way, in a more personal way. Without this experience, they are just another person telling you what to do. I take more notice of what she says now.' For another client, the club, from which weekends were organized, was seen as a favourable alternative to routine, office-based contact: 'Before I came on probation I thought it would just be a general talk about not getting into trouble with the police. There is a great deal of generosity here [the club]. They will sit and listen to you for hours. I know it is his job, but he looks interested in what you say.'

Adventure activities were not seen positively by all clients and officers, however. For one older man the need to sustain his relationship with his officer on a different basis served to confuse his perception of the probation officer as a professional social worker and authority figure. He found the combination of 'casualness' and 'authority' imposed by the adventure weekend setting difficult to unravel and cope with.

The place of adventure activities in the clients' lives

The interviews with clients also included reference to how activities organized by the probation service related to other aspects of their lives. Even those clients who had active social lives greatly valued the opportunity simply to get out of London for a while. This was particularly true of unsupported mothers and unemployed clients who found the cost of transport prohibitive. For about a third of the sample, however, the outings meant much more; in some cases they seemed to be the only pleasure in lonely, rather sad lives: 'Apart from Borstal, this is the only time I have ever been out of Battersea!' and 'Well, if it was not for these weekends, I would just be walking the streets not knowing what to do with myself.'

These statements, combined with the fact that very few clients organized further meetings or activities for themselves despite being very enthusiastic, illustrates that deprivation – educational, cultural and material – is a very real experience for many. Although the probation service brought individuals together as a group, it cannot sustain a group and eventually the clients are thrown back on to their own resources. For many, their financial or personal resources are simple insufficient to equip them for independent activity: 'Yes, I would go, but it's the finances and the transport, none of us at the club could afford a car or van to go in,' and 'I would not go away on my own, it's better going with a group. You need companionship.'

Involvement in the activities programme did act as a catalyst for some clients, however. They began to make fuller use of their local community facilities (i.e. swimming, football matches). It is important to note, however, that the clients who proved able to expand their interests tended to be those who had undertaken *several* activity weekends, indeed becoming involved with the planning and organization. In almost all cases these clients were attached to one of the probation clubs, which in fact makes it impossible to separate or identify which personal changes were due to activities and which to regular support derived from club membership.

The officers' view of the trips

It became evident from conversations with officers that they too found aspects of the ventures difficult. Their anxieties were rather different from the clients', however, and were centred around being responsible for the smooth running of the programme. According to many anecdotes, crises occasionally occurred (i.e. clients being arrested, getting lost or drunk, running away or being violent). When the officers' anxieties and experiences are looked at objectively, however, it becomes evident that two factors were commonly found to spark off incidents: (1) excess alcohol, and (2) an imbalanced mix of clients in terms of temperament and mental stability. Unlike clients' anxieties, which tend to fade with the number of trips undertaken, officers' anxiety levels in some cases seemed to remain constant. The continual vigilance required was described by one officer thus: 'I was talking to one kid on the trip about drinking and making trouble and he said I was paranoid. I agreed with him, but told him I had cause. As the weekend progressed, it became obvious that there would be no trouble, and I was able to relax.' It was not only the fear of something going wrong that caused stress, but simply being so exposed to the view of the clients, or as another officer described it: 'It is like living with mirrors on all sides, you can't escape a thing. Any remark you make will be taken up, and everything you do is seen by everyone else, no-one pulls any punches on weekends. But the nice thing is it is all coped with.'

Despite these feelings many officers took part repeatedly and talked with obvious pleasure of their clients' development and growth, which additionally renewed their faith in probation work:

The last two trips were so bad [clients' behaviour] that I began to have negative feelings about trips in general, but this one was so good it renewed my faith in trips and this job. It can really give you an injection of enthusiasm or faith in what you are doing. I think it is important to stress that point, how much good weekends do for POs [probation officers]. We come back and think, yes – it is an important job, and it *can* work.

Some differences between clients' and officers' views

The clients' discussions about the activities, while supporting much of what the probation officers said, also threw up some interesting differences. The most apparent was that clients did not perceive any connection between activities and improving relationship skills. Instead, they thought they were simply going canoeing or rock-climbing, and thus the activity was seen as an end in itself. Despite their not seeing the purpose of trips in officers' terms, it is interesting that one of the first issues that clients raised in interviews was pleasure and surprise at their forming social relationships, or, in their words, how everyone 'mucked in': 'Everyone was helping everyone else, no-one was left out. If someone didn't have anything or could not afford anything, someone else gave it to them', and 'We didn't mind having to do things like put tents up and that, everyone was pulling their weight.'

This is an important point, for several clients talked of their anxiety about the weekend before going: 'I wasn't too sure what it was going to be like, and the people worried me. I didn't know any of them, but I had a nice time', and 'I really had to pluck up my courage to go. Being with others I did not know scared me a lot.' It should be noted that some trips experienced a very high drop-out before departure, amounting to 75 per cent of clients in a few cases. This suggests that many clients are anxious about new experiences, particularly those in which they may fail and have that failure observed by strangers. For some, simply getting as far as the minibus could be regarded as something of an achievement.

Conclusion

This study set out to clarify probation officers' objectives behind the organization of adventure activities for their clients and to evaluate those activities from the stance of both the officer and client. It became clear very quickly that probation officers do not send their clients on adventure activities simply to learn a new skill or sport. While a broadening of the clients' horizons and a chance for them to enjoy themselves are frequently cited, the primary goal of the officers interviewed was for their clients to improve their skills with personal relationships. Adventure activities as a vehicle for improving these skills and increasing clients' (and at times officers') self-confidence would appear to be moderately successful. Several outings may be required, however, if the benefits are to be sustained and the clients able to transfer these new skills to their daily lives.

Such activities would also appear to be a useful way to facilitate the client/officer relationship. Several clients saw the probation service as a less rigid and more sympathetic organization following participation in adventure weekends. Additionally the shared experiences of clients and officers during the activity frequently enriched their relationship which, according to the clients, encouraged them to pay better attention to the officers' advice in subsequent office meetings. Finally, even if the home probation officer did not go on the trip, the activities introduced a new topic of conversation which seemed to revitalize office-based work for weeks after the event.

Adventure activities also appear to have the ability to meet the needs of a wide range of clients at different levels. At one level a weekend can simply be an interesting, pleasant one-off experience that can vitalize the probation officer and client relationship and be a welcome extra to continuing casework. For other clients – perhaps the less confident, those with a history of mental illness, and those with a propensity for violence – prolonged involvement can give both a tremendous confidence boost and provide a means for the longer-term improvement of social skills.

Two further issues emerged from the findings which organizers of similar activity programmes may find interesting. First, for some clients, the prospect of participating in activities causes considerable initial trepidation. This seems largely to be due to the fear of mixing with others, and thus several clients 'bottle out' and do not go on trips. Probably more clients could be encouraged to go if better preparation were undertaken by officers, particularly with anxious or withdrawn clients. Second, some clients who become regular 'trippers' have found it very difficult to move away from the sphere of the probation service and organize similar activities themselves. Many felt they lacked the financial resources and confidence to try. Organizers of activities programmes would do well to build in a 'moving on' component towards the end of programmes.

This paper may make adventure activities seem like a 'baptism of fire' for officers and clients; for some they are, but both parties benefit and seem to enjoy activities. For one officer who regularly went, adventure activities meant: 'You have to learn the techniques of this sort of venture as much as you have to learn any other type of social work. It is as hard and as complex as anything else we do.'

10

Help and Control in Probation: An Empirical Assessment of Probation Practice

Andrew Willis

In recent years a good deal of attention has been paid to the creation of new non-custodial sentences, especially those which might operate as alternatives to custody, whilst the continuing decline in the use of the probation order has gone largely unattended. This imbalance is redressed by presenting data from a small-scale survey of young adult male offenders on probation, using observations and tape-recordings of probation officer and client encounters in probation interviews, as well as comments about their experience of probation from both parties. Probation is shown as being primarily concerned with the direct provision of social welfare help or assistance for offenders and scarcely at all with matters of overt social control. These findings, which very closely mirror the non-treatment paradigm of probation practice proposed by Bottoms and McWilliams (1979), raise questions of principle and practice which are discussed.

Response to the probation crisis

One of the more alarming developments in penal policy in recent times is the increasing reluctance of the courts to award probation orders: the traditional non-custodial sanction of first resort. Although it was hailed in the 1950s as the most significant contribution to penal practice this century (Radzinowicz, 1958, x–xiv), we have witnessed a proportionate decline in its use since the 1930s, which accelerated in the 1950s (Barr and O'Leary, 1966) and the 1960s (Home Office, 1969). More recently, this trend has continued unabated. In 1978, for example, 26,706 persons aged 17 years or older were placed on probation compared with 27,633 in 1968 (Home Office, 1979a, table 5, 11), despite a 69 per cent increase in the volume of indictable crime and a 55 per cent increase in the numbers of offenders per 100,000 of the population in that period (Home Office, 1979c, table 1.2, 6, and table 3.2, 25). This spectacular upsurge in crime, it appears, is nothing like matched by an expansion in the award of probation. In fact, the reverse is true. Looking at the proportionate use of probation, whereas 14 per cent of young adult male and 7 per cent of adult male offenders convicted of indictable offences received probation orders in 1969, the proportions dropped to 7 per cent and 5 per cent, respectively, in 1979 (Home Office, 1980b, table 4.4, 42–3, and table 4.5, 46–7), a reduction in the use of probation of between one-quarter and one-half. Nor is there any comfort in more recent figures which, although they show a 20 per cent increase in the numbers of offenders awarded probation in 1980 over 1979 (Home Office, 1981c), also show that just 6 per cent of all convicted indictable offenders were given probation in 1980 compared with 13 per cent in 1970 (Home Office, 1981a, table 7.4, 153). The decline is real and continuing.

Part of the explanation for this lies in the way probation intervention has failed to have a significant impact on the criminality of offenders. It is now generally accepted that about 20 per cent of probation orders brought to a conclusion in any year will be for reasons other than good progress (Home Office, 1981c, table 11, 23), a roughly stable failure rate over the past 20 years (McClintock, 1958, Appendix 2, table 10, 69; Barr and O'Leary, 1966, table A, 14). Or, to put matters a rather different way, about 30 per cent of all probationers will reoffend within one year of the order being awarded (Folkard et al., 1976, tables 5 and 7, 17); though recent data with a follow-up period of six years point to a 63 per cent rate of reconviction (Phillpotts and Lancucki, 1979, table 3.1, 15). Clearly, as the Conference of Chief Probation Officers (1978) put it, the treatment model as practised has not produced the results its high priests promised, a conclusion echoed in all the comprehensive reviews of sentencing effectiveness (Lipton et al., 1975; Brody, 1976; Greenberg, 1977). Increased recognition of this fact has probably made probation progressively less attractive to sentencers.

Alongside this, deriving in part from critiques of custodial treatment (American Friends Service Committee, 1971; Von Hirsch, 1976), is the increasingly prominent view that the individual treatment model which underpins probation intervention is theoretically faulty. Bottoms and McWilliams argue, for example, that there is a misplaced analogy between crime and disease which does not permit anti-social conduct to be dealt with as if it were an illness. Moreover, to continue to coerce unwilling offenders to probation treatment is unjust in that it assumes a power over their lives out of all proportion to their wrongdoing; it is disingenuous because it ignores knowledge about the social rather than pathological causes of crime; and it is demeaning in that it treats clients as mere objects of penal policy to be manipulated at the whim of some therapeutic puppeteer (1979, 160–2, 168–72).

Taken together, these points present a serious challenge to established probation orthodoxy: declining rates, penal ineffectiveness and inappropriate use suggest a radical reconceptualization of probation practice may now be essential (Croft, 1978; Bottoms and McWilliams, 1979), and a number of attempts at philosophical reconstruction have been attempted. Parsloe (1979), for example, reaffirms the traditional duality of 'care' and 'control', pointing to the probation officer's equal social work obligation to offenders and crime prevention duty to the public. In contrast, Harris (1977, 1980) thinks the therapeutic-cum-punitive approach only offers the worst of both worlds: namely notional surveillance and compromised social work assistance. His solution is to dissociate treatment and punishment, and facilitate the former by means of a court-based social work service. Alternatively, Bottoms and McWilliams (1979) propose a non-treatment paradigm where the primary task would be to satisfy clients' demands for assistance by means of the substitution of help for treatment, and where the supervision of offenders would be the responsibility of the court. In contrast, others would see the future of probation in terms of socialist practice (Walker and Beaumont, 1981).

Interestingly, despite the varied character of these prescriptive responses to perceived crisis, what they have in common is that they are not grounded in recent empirical research in probation practice. It may be useful, therefore, to present some recent survey data which add an empirical dimension to a growing theoretical debate. As some commentators have put it, the only way forward in social work (except to drift) is to examine practice from the roots up, to find out what actually happens at present in social worker/client encounters as a necessary prelude to reforming professional practice (Brewer and Lait, 1980, chapter 10; Bagshaw, 1981).

To this end, in 1979 the author conducted a survey of the probation experience of 30 male clients and their supervising officers during the initial six weeks of probation. The researcher attended as an observer and tape-recorded the first two probation interviews. In addition, immediately after such interviews, the probation officer and client were separately asked a series of open-ended questions inviting subjects to describe and evaluate the recently completed probation interview, as well as to comment in more general terms about their probation hopes and fears. This double-barrelled research strategy was designed to provide a documentary record of what actually went on in probation intervention and to measure the congruence (or lack of it) between probation officers' and clients' perceptions of it. Throughout, it was simply assumed as axiomatic that subjects had an unqualified right to comment on their situations and that their remarks should be taken seriously (Harré and Secord, 1976, chapter 6).

Before presenting the survey findings, it is important to stress the typicality of the sample of offenders. Their average age was 21 years, with three-quarters aged 17–20 years. In all bar three cases the probation order was made following a social inquiry report, and all of those contained a positive probation recommendation. The majority of orders were for two years and they were awarded mainly for the acquisitive crimes of burglary, theft and taking motor vehicles, and usually on a first or second court appearance. Against this, though, clients owed an average £123 by way of outstanding fines or compensation, despite the fact that two-thirds had no more than one previous conviction. Finally, over half were unemployed at the time the probation order was made.

Given the rather probing nature of the research design as it entered the intimacy and privacy of the probation officer/client relationship, what sort of data could be anticipated? Would the balance of probation intervention tilt towards crime control through surveillance (Advisory Council on the Penal System, 1974); social welfare help or assistance (Bottoms and McWilliams, 1979); or a subtle blend of both (Parsloe, 1979)? And given the flexible, open-ended, interrogative research style, just how would subjects view this intervention? Would clients see probation mainly in terms of unwarranted interference with their liberties (Giller and Morris, 1978; Davies, 1979), or in social work terms (Harris, 1977)? And, if the latter, would it be viewed as genuine (Bottoms and McWilliams, 1979), or as inappropriate and misguided (Meyer and Timms, 1970; Morris and Beverly, 1975, chapter 7)? So the existing literature suggested any number of quite different and fascinating possibilities, though all that was important at this stage was that any sensible and constructive development of probation policy should be predicated on an empirical survey of actual probation practice.

Control versus help in probation

The most striking feature of the probation interviews was the minimal concern with what might be termed the formal or social control aspects of probation supervision. For example, in one-third of the cases the probation order itself was not discussed or explained to clients; in a further one-third it was but briefly explained; and in only the final one-third did officers paraphrase and explain the requirements of the order in any detail. Very surprisingly, then, in a high proportion of cases the most obvious strategy for stressing the surveillance and crime-prevention aspect of probation was ignored. In addition, breach proceedings were mentioned in only one in six of the cases, and then only very briefly without any attempt to paraphrase into non-technical language. On top of this, in as many as 50 per cent of the cases there was no reference made in the first two probation interviews either to the instant offence or to previous criminal misbehaviour. Criminality, it appears, was often seen as a rather unimportant and inconsequential topic of conversation. It really did not figure to any significant extent, though when it did the focus was very clearly on crime prevention (strategies to avoid the perceived need to engage in dishonesty, etc.) rather than individual deterrence (threats of loss of liberty). Almost all the features of probation, which would normally be associated as necessary components of upholding the law and protecting society by way of imposing on offenders the discipline of submission to supervision (Home Office, 1978b, para. 52, 16–17), were conspicuously absent. The sheer scale of these omissions suggests far more than simply large-scale inadvertence or massively sloppy probation practice. What is implied is a measured or calculated rejection of overt social control as a superordinate probation goal.

What, then, did comprise probation intervention if coercive threats and naked surveillance were so glaringly absent? Content analysis of probation interviews revealed that officers' energies were mainly directed towards a traditional and official aim of probation, namely that of providing clients with 'help in difficulties over money, accommodation or employment' (Home Office, 1978b, para. 53, 17). In each of these areas officers addressed themselves in a direct and practical fashion to a range of everyday problems and difficulties, and suggested, promised or delivered on-the-spot action which would lead to remedy or afford relief. The business of probation, it appeared, was all about the provision of help.

In the 18 cases where the offender was unemployed, for example, the practical question of his finding and obtaining work was attended to in every case. In a few instances this took the form of some fairly stern advice about the court's or officer's expectation that the offender obtain work even though this prove difficult. But in the vast majority of cases it involved practical assistance rather than verbal exhortation. Officers used their informal contacts to arrange job interviews in the private and public sector and with respect to government training schemes. Frequently, these had been arranged in advance of the very first probation interview, or had been set up as appointments to be kept immediately afterwards. In both, officers would very often accompany clients and speak on their behalf. In addition, many offenders were offered coaching in their presentational style at these job interviews by means of advice, encouragement or social skills training: offers which were never declined by clients. Overall, despite the seemingly intractable nature of the unemployment problem, there was compelling evidence of large-scale, practical attempts on the part of probation officers to find work for offenders.

Alongside this, a good deal of effort was directed towards the financial circumstances of clients. In the majority of cases they were questioned about the general state of their finances and their ability to cope on what was often an extremely limited income, and in about one-quarter of these some difficulties (actual income or money management) emerged.

In all these cases, discussion then moved beyond simple interrogation ('How much money do you get? How well do you manage?') and clients were offered practical advice on ways to improve their financial position or alleviate pressing difficulties. This took the form of practical advice on saving, budgeting more adequately, or obtaining maximum State benefits. All this was down-to-earth and practical, something a long way distant from the moral imperatives of the Protestant ethic of work and deferred gratification. Further, in nearly half of the 20 cases where offenders owed monies to the court, with an average debt of £123, probation officers took immediate steps to facilitate offenders paying by instalments, or arranged for multiple fines to be paid at a single court. Again, even in an area where there was singularly little room for manoeuvre, the emphasis was on help.

There was also overwhelming evidence that officers paid particular attention to probationers' domestic difficulties, which mainly centred on accommodation problems, or intra-familial disputes. These sorts of difficulties emerged in about two-thirds of the cases, and each and every one of them gave rise to a problem-solving approach on the part of probation officers, including: advice on how to minimize or avoid persistent quarrelling at home; social skills training to combat a client's chronic embarrassment at meeting other people; sex education; securing the return of clients' material goods; and, with respect to accommodation, direct assistance with the local authority, housing association or probation hostel. Clearly, although the precise nature of the intervention was quite different in each of these cases, what they had in common was immediate action (rather than mere words or advice) intended to bring real relief.

There can be no doubt that when these examples are taken in aggregate, the primary and almost exclusive emphasis in probation was in the provision of direct social work assistance or help. In terms of what actually went on during the initial probation encounters, relief of need was clearly superordinate to the explicit control of criminal behaviour. Just as the absence of individual deterrent elements suggests an attenuated concern for crime control, the sheer preponderance of straightforward practical assistance confirms the relief of need as the primary probation goal.

Comments from clients

These data, though, give an incomplete account of probation. They provide a documentary record of what actually happened in the probation officer/client encounters, but they do not begin to unravel the way in which subjects themselves (officers and clients) perceive and evaluate them. This was done by means of a range of open-ended questions (put separately to both parties in the probation dyad) asking them to define the probationer's problems, describe the nature of their experience of probation, comment on what probation was trying to do and evaluate the best of probation. In effect, these constituted a series of open-ended invitations to comment on probation. It was seen as a methodological strength that subjects should have the maximum opportunity possible to express themselves in a natural and uninhibited fashion without the artificial constraints imposed by a fixed-choice questionnaire.

In the first of these areas subjects were simply asked what, if anything, appeared to them as the major or principal problems facing that particular client? Interestingly in 23, or 77 per cent, of the cases the two parties responded in an identical or near-identical fashion, despite the fact that each was unaware of the other's response. Also the framing of the question gave no possible guide as to how the answer should be phrased, and neither officer nor client had much knowledge of the other, having only just concluded their initial probation interview. In most of these cases there was a very clear and definite emphasis on practical problems. This high level of concordance is best illustrated by juxtaposing some responses:[1]

C   The main problems are financial.

PO   The primary problems that come to mind are finance and sorting out of debts. (Case 6)

C   Well, housing and work.

PO   Well, there's the housing situation ... There's also this employment thing. (Case 10)

C   Me and my wife arguing and she wants to try and put a stop to it.

PO   The marriage ... definitely. The matrimonial situation between them. (Case 11)

C   Finding a place.

PO   Well, his principal problem is accommodation. (Case 13)

C   My debts. They're the main problem, like. The money.

PO   Well, on a practical basis there's the money management problem. (Case 16)

C   The drink.

PO   The drink. (Case 27)

C   My job ... Getting a job.

PO   Well, unemployment. (Case 30)

Probation intervention, then, appeared to be largely predicated on the mutual identification by probation officer and client of a range of down-to-earth problems facing clients. Abstract problems such as immaturity or inadequacy were seldom mentioned by probation officers and never mentioned by clients. This congruence of view is important because it stands in contrast to earlier research which found a continuous tug o'war between client and social worker: the former continuously trying to direct attention to material needs which the latter saw as simply a return to presenting problems (Meyer and Timms, 1970, chapter 7). In the penal field, work on parolees and probationers has suggested that offenders' conceptions of welfare needs were considered by officers to be both unwanted and inappropriate, largely because many problems (such as debt, unemployment, domestic tension) were so ubiquitous as to be regarded as normal (Davies, 1974a, chapter 7; Morris and Beverly, 1975, chapter 7). But in this survey there was no evidence whatsoever of these oppositional perspectives. On the contrary, both parties independently determined problem areas in identical terms.

This view receives considerable support when the descriptive and evaluative comments from clients are taken into account. These reinforce the view that probation can be seen as a largely collaborative exercise between officers and clients focusing on the relief of need. When clients were asked after each of the first two probation interviews: 'What was going on in the interview? Can you describe to me what happened? What was the probation officer trying to do?', as many as 80 per cent of them replied in the unambiguous vocabulary of problem specific help, as the following examples illustrate:

She said she was going to help me get a job by seeing if I could go on that course. (Case1)

All about working (...) To keep me out of trouble and to get me a job. She was doing the right thing. (Case 5)

To sort things out up at the house. (Case 8)

And he asked me about accommodation. And he had helped me and he did phone them about the delay on their side with the housing. (Case 10)

Trying to help me (...) Trying to put me on my feet and trying to help me with my court case (...) I appreciated that a lot, like. (Case 15)

All about my job and how he can help us out. (Case 19)

Well, he was trying to help us (...) Trying to help me get a new job. (Case 20)

Well, he says he'll try and stop me arguing with my old man (...) And to try and get me a job. (Case 25)

And, interestingly, when the same type of question was put to probation officers, more than half also chose to describe probation in terms of the provision of social welfare assistance.

In order to check on the above perceptions, at the end of the survey period clients were asked: 'What do you think your probation officer has been trying to do during the last six weeks?'; and officers were asked: 'What have you been trying to do during the last six weeks?' This type of question invited subjects to describe probation in more general terms rather than recount what they thought had happened in a single probation interview. In three-quarters of the cases subjects agreed in their overall description of probation, and in the majority of cases they opined that probation was about practical assistance. In fact, some 80 per cent of the clients chose to use the words 'help' or 'assistance' or like terms, to sum up their view on the nature of probation intervention. Again, these points are best illustrated by juxtaposing some replies from officers and clients:

PO First of all to get the accommodation problem sorted out.

C Well, I know he's tried to help me get a house, you know. (Case 11)

PO Pursuing employment through the medium of the Coal Board.

C Help me in trying to get a job. (Case 12).

PO It started off very well because he fitted in on our Social Skills course.

C He's helped (. . .) He took me on that course thing and it taught me how to look for a job. That's helped me. (Case 13)

PO Well (. . .) perhaps he's got somebody he can come along to when he's in a bit of a mess.

C I find, in fact that he's a great help. I find that if anything bugs me, he'll sort it out for me . . . straight. Like with the HP problem. (Case 16)

PO Helping him with his search for a job.
C Well, trying to help me get on. He's been trying to help me get a job. (Case 20)

PO Looking at the family problems. Looking at the father's DHSS benefits ... And looking at the house.
C He was going to try and get our family a new house, you know (...) He's been helpful. (Case 21)

PO Making efforts to find him a job.
C He's been trying to help me get a job and things like that. And sort things out with me girl and the baby, like. (Case 22)

PO Basically, look at the family problems and the job.
C Trying to get everything sorted out with the home and all that. Trying to get me a job (...) I'm very pleased. (Case 24)

Moreover, when clients were explicitly asked to put a value on the probation intervention received to date by means of the question: 'What so far do you see as the most rewarding and useful part of probation?', over 50 per cent responded in terms of the unambiguous language of help, as these examples suggest:

It is helpful to sort my problems out and to try and find me a place. (Case 1)

If any problems arose, the probation officer he can do something about it (...) He's got a bit of pull. (Case 10)

Trying to get me a job, I think. He's helped me a lot there (...) I'm happy I had it you know, probation. I'm very grateful to him. (Case 13)

I'm very happy. He's said he'll try and get me a job. (Case 20)

Trying to get me a job (...) He has helped me, like. (Case 22)

He's helped me back at home (...) That's what's helped me. (Case 24)

Well, he's helpful in every way. (Case 27)

He's helped me a bit more about sex. (Case 28)

All of it (...) it's all been beneficial. (Case 29)

Clearly, throughout the survey period, whenever clients were asked to describe or evaluate probation they chose to do so in terms of help or the provision of social welfare assistance, and never in terms of social control. Very largely, probation officers shared this perspective.

Finally, and unexpectedly, although the survey was not designed to explore the extent to which clients valued being in a position to 'talk things over' with their supervising officers, at various points throughout the survey, clients said that what they liked about probation and saw as valuable was that it offered them a welcome opportunity to share a personal problem, or simply have a chat with a sympathetic listener. Overall some 80 per cent of the clients made spontaneous comments of this type. 'Having a chat' was seen as a valuable end in itself, especially with someone outside the family who could be relied upon to listen patiently. A few of their comments quoted below illustrate the range and strength of these unsolicited views:

We sit down and talked things over, like. I enjoyed the talking (...) She's very understanding (...) It's like a break with myself to talk with somebody else (...) I feel better after talking to her. It's better, see, after talking to outsiders. (Case 5)

It's nice to come along and chat to someone, you know. It's like as though you're going to visit a friend (...) As a person I like her (...) You can talk to her and she doesn't mind. (Case 6)

And to tell you the truth, it's nice to come down and have a break, you know, and talk things over. That's what I think.

I know I shouldn't say it but I think I'll enjoy coming down here for a year, like. (Case 11)

Sitting and talking. It makes me feel relaxed (. . .) It allows me to talk about my problems with him (. . .) Nobody else seems to listen. I've got my mother and my father but they don't seem to care so much. He's the only one who seems to care. He's the only one who'll listen. (Case 17)

Talking to him kind of makes me feel better. It gets things off my mind (. . .) He kind of makes me feel better. He kind of takes a lot of pressure off me. (Case 20)

I come in and talk to him, like, and it take a lot off my mind, like (. . .) He listens to my problems (. . .) You need someone like him (. . .) And you can talk to him and he's not going to shout and scream, is he? Like, you haven't got to bottle it up inside you. (Case 27)

He's good (. . .) Good at understanding. He listens to all the problems. (Case 28)

Issues and implications

Considering these data as a whole, it is clear that there is little or no support for the fairly common view of probation as a subtle blend of social control and social welfare (Hunt, 1964; Parsloe, 1976, 1979). It is quite inaccurate to think of contemporary probation practice as an ideal combination of individual deterrence and rehabilitation, as something which both protects society and strengthens offenders' own resources (Home Office, 1978b, para. 52, 17). We can also reject other more-or-less official conceptions of probation officers providing 'caring authority' (Parsloe, 1979), or 'supportive surveillance' (Singer, 1980). Rather the balance in practice shifts decisively in favour of help over control, with formal supervision assuming, at best, a markedly residual role. Equally, there is no support for a psychotherapeutic model of probation, one with an emphasis on 'interpretive and therapeutic techniques within the confines of a one-to-one relationship' (Davies, 1974b, 134). Neither are there grounds for assuming that probation has anything to do with the promotion of understanding or insight by means of non-directive discussions (Folkard et al., 1966). The whole notion of a dynamic interaction of attitudes and emotions between officer and client, with the purpose of helping the client achieve a better adjustment (Biestek, 1957), seems singularly out of place. Perhaps, as Baroness Wootton put it some years ago, the social worker simply has no need to pose as a miniature psychoanalyst if the simple provision of straightforward help is seen as a legitimate professional activity in its own right (1959, 296).

What is suggested is that demands for casework and for overt forms of social control have been ousted by the dynamics of need. Probation is primarily concerned with bringing relief and service to clients whose circumstances might have otherwise appeared to them intolerable (Harris, 1977; Rees, 1978). As such, it is an individualized approach to need rather than an individualized approach to crime. Content analysis of actual probation interviews and comments from clients both confirm the validity of the non-treatment paradigm of Bottoms and McWilliams. The authors redirect attention, in the light of the limitations of the treatment model, towards the traditional aim of the probation service: assisting offenders. They also stress the importance of a client-centred approach being premised both on shared assessment and on an unconditional offer of help (1979, 172–4). Simply put, but not overstating the case, clients and officers alike see probationers' problems almost exclusively in terms of everyday domestic, financial and employment difficulties: these (and not crime) are the sole focus of actual intervention; and this social work assistance is something clients both want and appreciate. And it is also worth stressing, to strengthen these conclusions and to forestall any possible criticism that somehow these data were inadvertently contaminated in the light of the Bottoms and

McWilliams paradigm, that the research design and data collection preceded publication of their non-treatment model. Actual probation practice, therefore, may well have been one step ahead of theoretical attempts at reformulation.

It is also worth noting that this sort of approach may well constitute a rational, moral and acceptable response to crime, and one which reflects certain traditional probation virtues. To begin with, it is an enduring and explicit aim in probation to make available to clients skilled help to cope with money, accommodation or employment difficulties (Home Office, 1978b, paras 52, 53, 16–17), a view reflected in influential probation studies (Davies, 1974b; Folkard et al., 1976). It is a reasonable response because, as Bottoms and McWilliams point out (1979, 174, 175), there is little evidence that probation-as-help is either more or less effective in the prevention of crime than more traditional approaches. It is moral because it recognizes, or even insists, on the full moral autonomy of offenders and has no truck with coercion to treatment. And it is acceptable – at least to clients and their supervising officers – for this, after all, is how they choose to engage in probation.

It is also true, however, that a more widespread and formal endorsement of such a model (probation-as-help-as-a-matter-of-policy rather than probation-as-help-by-stealth which is a grass-roots, almost underground, response to the collapse of confidence in the treatment model) is fraught with difficulties. It is by no means certain that, at a formal level, the downgrading of social control to a point of virtual insignificance would prove acceptable: to governments, the probation service itself, or to the general public. This would certainly be at odds with part of the official Home Office rhetoric which talks of a fundamental aim in probation as being 'to uphold the law and protect society ... through the discipline of submission to supervision' (Home Office, 1978b, para. 52, 16). Even Bottoms and McWilliams fight shy of endorsing help to the exclusion of control, with a significant portion of their essay being concerned with outlining a court-based mechanism of statutory supervision. They are adamant, for example, that the community has a legitimate wish for discipline of this sort and they see the law enforcement role in probation as an enduring feature which cannot be evaded (1979, 175–9). It is one thing to propose the substitution of help for treatment, but quite another to suggest the substitution of help for social control. Political realism probably dictates that probation is underwritten by explicit recognition of its crime control function. This way it continues to distinguish between the needs of the offender, which are met by help, and the seriousness of the offence, which is marked by an element of social control.

This point assumes additional significance as penal policy increasingly seeks to locate a greater proportion of convicted persons in the non-custodial range of sentences. Any success in displacing the less tractable sort of offender from custody – irrespective of whether this is a product of genuine preferment of non-custodial over institutional options, or a more expedient response to an overburdened prison system – is probably conditional on a toughening-up of community supervision. If the sum total of penal misery is to stay the same, then those offenders displaced from custody must receive additional penal discomforts in the community in order to compensate for their not being deprived of their liberty. The proposal from the Advisory Council on the Penal System (1974, paras 19–21, 5–6, and paras 42–8, 12–13) for a 'supervision and control order' to replace probation for young adult offenders, for example, explicitly provided for 'close' and 'strict' community control over and above the 'customary' levels as the necessary price to pay for avoiding committals to custody. And, in more recent times, the same kind of logic is probably at work in the experimental Medway Centre in Kent, in night restriction or curfew options, and the overall objectives underlying the Criminal Justice Act 1982. It is not without significance that even within the probation service it is now being argued that this trade-off between increased community supervision by means of control and surveillance is a necessary and desirable price to pay for reducing committals to custody (Griffiths, 1982a, 1982b), although it is by no means a one-sided argument (Lacey et al., 1983).

Keeping people out of prison may mean that probation is allowed to cross the line from supervised freedom to a form of custody in the community. In fact, as pressures on a grossly overburdened prison system give added impetus to the decarceration movement, this drift towards a toughening-up of community supervision may prove inexorable. This would mean that probation-as-help could never be more than an 'elaborate pretence' (Fisher, 1978).

Alongside this, there is a further difficulty with probation officers' professional self-image were they to accept and endorse the non-treatment model as an established part of probation orthodoxy. If probation officers' efforts were to be concentrated in the areas identified in the survey (low-key, practical, down-to-earth assistance with money, accommodation and employment problems), then questions could be raised about whether this sort of service could not just as well be provided by persons without a long and expensive professional social work training (such as voluntary associates) as by probation officers. After all, the skills required appear to be concrete, practical and worldly, and not really in any way diagnostic or having a casework orientation. And the sort of model of practice which is implied here – a small number of professionally qualified officers overseeing a large number of less well-trained colleagues or volunteers, who then have the bulk of the contact with clients – is not at all far fetched. In Australia and North America, for example, voluntary supervisors play an important role, whilst in Sweden they are the cornerstone of criminal supervision (Whitfield, 1980). In this country, too, when full-time ancillary workers and sessional supervisors on community service schemes comprise as many as 18 per cent of the total persons in the probation service having regular contact with clients (Home Office, 1981c, chapter 10), the trend towards the para-professional probation officer is pretty clear. What is not clear, though, at this juncture, is whether the service would welcome the help model if, at the same time, this could lead to the progressive downgrading of its professional status. Equally officers may feel unwilling to subscribe to a type of supervision which would be a good deal more visible and open to scrutiny than more traditional practices. The non-treatment paradigm suggests a cafeteria style of probation, one where clients, so to speak, view services on display, assess them and are then free to accept or reject them. One consequence of this is that both the take-up and rejection of help would become very much more visible, something which would work to the advantage of those officers who successfully provided the assistance clients wanted, but would also make public the lack of service or disservice of their less capable colleagues. No doubt, as Bottoms and McWilliams intend, this bottom-up monitoring would improve the service to clients, but it is by no means certain that officers would want this if, at the same time, it made their activities (and inactivities) that much more visible and accountable. So fear of a diminution of professional status and concern over public scrutiny of poor social work performance would tend to militate against probation-officer endorsement of the help model.

These difficulties aside, what is abundantly clear from the survey data is that the traditional probation order, albeit with a new emphasis, still has a significant role to play in community-based corrections. It may no longer merit the pre-eminence it once had and it may not prove at all suitable for the more serious or repetitive offender, but some offenders need help and this it can provide. Where Bottoms and McWilliams pointed towards the desirability of a non-treatment ethic in probation, the data presented above point towards its operational feasibility.

NOTES

1 In presenting material from the tape-recorded probation interviews the following conventions have been adopted:

...	pause;
(...)	material edited out;
PO	Probation Officer;
C	Client.

11

Conclusion: Some Implications for Social Work Agencies

Ian Butler

Others in this volume have considered the peripheral role occupied by 'alternatives to custody' in relation to broader social and penal policy (Pointing, chapter 1; Willis, chapter 2). It is difficult to imagine progress being made at the policy level, however, unless equal consideration is given to 'alternative' methods of work and to how these can be integrated with existing social work theory and practice. This is because the initiation and delivery of alternatives to custody occur within social work organizations rather than in distinct settings having a direct connection to penal policy. This situation helps to explain the marginality of many alternatives to sentencers. Moreover, scepticism as to the benefits of alternatives amongst sentencers may well stem from the accurate observation that such initiatives seem to be peripheral to the mainstream work of the agency presenting them. My purpose in this final chapter is to explore the uncertain status of alternatives to custody in relation to some features of current social work practice.

Social work's stock in trade is change and the management of change. How unfortunate, therefore, that as a profession it should have such difficulties in accommodating or promoting change within itself. Some of these difficulties derive from the organizational context in which social work services are delivered. This is the same organizational framework as that developing alternatives to custody, namely social service departments of the local authority and probation departments. These agencies are described, following Dorothy Smith (1965, 381–99), as 'front line organisations'. Such organizations, it is argued, appear to function hierarchically, operating along well understood line-management principles with strongly central-ized procedures for decision making and policy formulation.

However, as each service is largely composed of profes-sionally trained people, individually responsible for their actions and relying on personal judgement, such a description proves unreliable. In fact, one finds real executive power and decision making dispersed amongst those at some distance from the centre, amongst those on the 'front line'. In effect, field social workers, probation officers, IT units and other front-line units are able to recreate and redefine agency policy and practice by the way in which they decide to order priorities, initiate new work and set objectives in their day-to-day work with clients.

Front-line units, it is suggested, can acquire a high degree of autonomy, allowing them to shape the development of specialist interests and particular expertise. The paradox of this kind of front-line autonomy is that while it permits the creation and small-scale implementation of innovatory methods of working, such as an alternative to custody, the opportunity for their wider promulgation and proper coor-dination is severely restricted. A front-line unit may choose to restrict the circulation of information resulting from its work in order to protect its autonomy. Moreover, other front-line units are similarly able to resist outside influences. There is no reason to assume that the difficulties posed by operational autonomy are more likely to be resolved if the initiative originates in the apex of the hierarchy, since this would still involve the front line presenting the work in a particular or selective light.

Front-line autonomy is not usually complete. Public accountability, as well as the operational need to curtail ambiguity in service delivery, ensures that for the organizational 'parent' of a front-line unit the main problem is one of maintaining control. As Gilbert Smith (1979, 37) notes: 'This dilemma is solved by attempts to strengthen the pattern of operational control and reduce the autonomy of front line units.' In other words, there is a strong organizational incentive for the 'parent' of a front-line unit to stifle aberrations from current policy and practice and to preserve the *status quo*, further militating against the integration of alternatives to custody with existing practice. Smith goes on to explain that normative professional training and control over information flows (e.g. minutes of meetings circulating selected and uncontentious information up the hierarchy) further atrophy innovation.

More subtly, the 'therapeutic' supervision of front-line staff by senior colleagues produces a climate in which opportunities to exercise control and stifle innovation are created. Gilbert Smith's discussion of professional norms is useful here. He describes the resolution of conflicting norms by reference to: 'organisational rules which apparently harm clients [being] . . . placed within the context of a theory in which they are justified in terms of client welfare' (1979, 37). This can lead, for example, to the almost totally unhelpful experience of early rising, kit cleaning, daily showers and drill being defined as providing a structured environment needed by young people, rather than being seen as nothing more than an emanation of a custodial philosophy.

Besides internal organizational factors, there are interorganizational rivalries to consider in understanding the difficulties of establishing alternative provisions to custody. In the case of young offenders, there remain serious discrepancies as to which agency has the clients and which the resources to fund programmes. As was recently argued in the Short Report: 'Local authorities provide most of the facilities and hitherto most of the funds, although projects are also set up by voluntary bodies, the probation service and others. In Staffordshire for example the Committee heard of cumbersome financial arrangements which made it quite unnecessarily difficult for the probation service to set up IT schemes' (Social Services Committee, 1984, para. 64).

In emphasizing structural and organizational factors there is the danger of forgetting the human dimension. Imagine yourself as the keeper of some embattled fortress (a probation department, say). It is hard enough to ward off the demands of the folk clamouring at your gates and to keep the paperwork flowing. Someone then comes along and suggests digging an escape tunnel. What will appear to the few as a solution to the problem will appear to others as yet another piece of work to be undertaken, and is there not enough to do already? Where keeping pace is a problem, which the ever-rising throughput of offenders ensures, changing direction appears an impossibility. Furthermore, elevating the important at the expense of the urgent requires degrees of imagination and courage which are rarely found in any organization.

Another human factor inhibiting the development of alternatives to custody concerns the unattractiveness of the client group. As noted by Harraway (chapter 4), those clients most likely to benefit in penological terms are not necessarily the same as those whom social workers want on their caseloads. As Harraway suggests, if social workers' discretion to recommend custody is curtailed, then the 'out of sight' drawer in one's mental filing cabinet is forced open, and serious work with difficult clients must begin. However, before changing the ways in which social inquiry reports are written (cf. Willis, chapter 2), a social worker has to convince him- or herself that he or she wants to work with more difficult clients, and in new and perhaps untried ways.

The various contributions to this book point the way to the development of social work practice in relation to the management of offending. The book contributes also to the development of social work theory in its insistence that workable alternative programmes must give higher priority to the point of view of clients. But disturbing the dust on the volumes of Florence Hollis that still lurk in too many area offices presents a formidable task. Willis (chapter 10) has described how that most familiar of social work relationships, the one developed in the privacy of one's own office, has altered to arrive at a more pragmatic and problem-solving approach. I wonder how calmly the mystery of the craft has been surrendered and how widely it has been accomplished. Cleaving social workers from their methodology may prove more difficult, and especially in a profession where so little, both in terms of resources and support, is devoted to post-qualifying training.

I began this chapter by suggesting that part of the estrangement of alternatives to custody from essential penal policy can be traced to the distance between such alternatives and the actual practice of social work. The impediments to development and integration that I have adduced here, such as a high degree of 'ad hocery', organizational inertia, the threat of the new, etc., could in principle be overcome; but only if one could be sure that a desire to overcome them existed. The lack of any great will to find a way forward is related, I believe, to the enormous scale of the change that alternatives to custody require. This has only partly been appreciated in the social work field but, just as crucially, the need for change is almost totally ignored outside it.

Webster's dictionary defines an alternative as a: 'choice between two things so that if one is taken the other must be left, a possibility of one of two things so that if one is false the other must be true'. Hence in postulating an alternative strategy for the management of offenders, logically one is discarding one option in preference to another, not merely accommodating a variation. That is to say that the creation of alternatives to custody postulates the dismantling not only of a great deal of the heavy plant currently in use within the penal system (some of which resides within the social work empire), but it also implies an assault on the ideologies which sustain current practice.

Our discussion to date has mainly focused on the difficulties of getting a new idea into someone's head. These difficulties are as nothing compared to those of getting an old one out, especially one so old and venerated as that which sustains the institutionally-orientated penal policies of the current age. As Millham writes of young people and the residential tradition:

it is a very strong tradition. It has been going on for nearly 300 years and is not going to be shifted by a few murmurs about IT, particularly when children are often popped into institutions by an adminstrative elite who have been educated in similar places and whose idea of adolescent heaven is a whiff of lifebuoy soap and a sweaty sock. (1981, 14)

Jerome Miller's experience in Massachusetts is a further indication of the scale and source of the opposition that can be expected if one pursues the logic of alternatives to custody, not least from those employed in residential and penal establishments, and having vested interests in them. Miller fully appreciated the power of the custody lobby, and largely for this reason decided to close down custodial institutions before appropriate alternatives were set up. In a recent article, Rutherford (1984) acknowledged that even Miller's critics (including liberals) had conceded that a gradualist approach would have failed. It would be tempting to make the point that a similarly radical approach is needed in Britain. However, the political climate in Britain today, the caution of the Civil Service and the power of a largely Conservative legal establishment, gravitate away from even the most modest modifications to penality. In this country moreover, even when well-established alternatives are available, these tend to be used in addition to custodial facilities rather than in place of them. As a result, alternatives to custody tend to be used as alternatives to supervision or other lower tariff disposals, as documented by Thorpe and others (Thorpe et al., 1980; Thorpe, 1983).

Perhaps it is not surprising, in view of the weak position of alternatives to custody in relation to penal policy, that a majority of social workers are less than enthusiastic about developing alternative programmes. More prosaically, any championing for alternatives puts them in an awkward position in court. Fineman and Eden analyse this issue in terms of the role implications for probation officers. A probation officer is a person who:

> ought to be keeping people out of prison; ought not to be just a servant of the court, but be negotiating with the court on behalf of his client; ought to be cultivating and supporting resources to help offenders learn and adjust to living in the community . . .

For many officers this new role was potentially very threatening and indeed *contrary to their own conception of what they ought to be doing.* Their customary behaviour with the courts would be to complete a 'social inquiry' report on the offender and, ultimately, leave the onus of responsibility for a decision concerning the client with the court. (1979, 33) [my italics]

Social work agencies, at least those operating within the framework of the local state, cannot claim a long or glorious tradition as agents of social development. It is not difficult to see why. As subservient participants in the courts system, they have neither the mandate nor the incentive to take on a radical stance. It is necessary to broaden debate on criminal justice policy considerably for a successful attack to be sustained against custodial provision. Social work's role in this is important, but alone it lacks clout. But social work organizations, in offering alternatives, must demonstrate logical consistency in their programmes. Even in this volume one has to assume a greater homogeneity between contributions than is actually the case. For example, the significance of the criminal act, either for understanding the offender or as an issue helping to decide what form of appropriate action to take, varies considerably between projects. As well as the need for greater coherence, more consideration is needed about which clients should be decarcerated and which should not be. Such issues cannot be decided behind the closed doors of any professional or other group acting alone. A much broader impetus to reform is required than that engendered by social work. Pearson offers some hope in this, in comparing reform with reaction based on punitive force:

As matters are usually stated, reform is equated with weakness, while its opponent is imbued with virile strength ... It is reaction that is an admission of weakness, in that the refusal to enter into dialogue and to attempt to persuade wrongdoers that there are good and tangible reasons why they should lead good and useful lives is tantamount to a failure of faith in the system of rewards, regulation and law itself. Weakness, not strength, lies behind the command that reformative principles of 'willing obedience' should be relinquished in favour of the 'short, sharp shock'. (1983, 238)

This volume constitutes a step towards changing the custodial focus of penal policy. It argues for the development of a more complex and difficult system, organized around reformative principles but allowing tangible benefits to be gained by offenders. This book also makes clear that controls over offenders' behaviour need to be built into alternative-to-custody programmes, since otherwise these will lack credibility with courts and the public in general, and leave offenders in much the same position as before. Finally, it is clear from the programmes considered that experiment, risk taking and innovation are needed in running custodial alternatives. Should this path not be followed, then the present situation of many offenders – of being trapped in a 'revolving door' relationship to prison – can only deteriorate further.

Bibliography

Advisory Council on the Penal System (1970) *Report on Non-Custodial and Semi-Custodial Penalties (Wootton Report)*. London: HMSO.

Advisory Council on the Penal System (1974) *Young Adult Offenders*. London: HMSO.

Advisory Council on the Penal System (1977) *Interim Report: The Length of Prison Sentences*. London: HMSO.

Advisory Council on the Penal System (1978) *Sentences of Imprisonment: A Review of Maximum Penalties*. London: HMSO.

American Friends Service Committee (1971) *Struggle for Justice*. New York: Hill & Wang.

American Medical Association (1977) *Manual on Alcoholism*. Chicago, Illinois: AMA Publications.

Anderson, R., Bulos, M. A. and Walker, S. R. (1985) *Tower Blocks*. London: Institute of Housing/Polytechnic of the South Bank.

Archard, P. and Cook, T. (1974) *Pilot Study of Alcoholics Recovery Project Shopfronts in 1972*. London: ARP Occasional Publications.

Bagshaw, P. (1981) Review of H. Walker and B. Beaumont (1981) *Probation Work: Critical Theory and Socialist Practice*, Oxford: Blackwell, in *Probation Journal*, 28, 3, 75–6.

Bailey, R. (1979) 'The reduction of pressure on the prison system', in unpublished *Report of the Conference held on 15th. June 1979 to discuss the House of Commons Expenditure Commitee Report*.

Barnard, E. and Bottoms, A. E. (1979) 'Facilitating Decisions not to Imprison', in *The Petty Persistent Offender*, 17–27. London: NACRO.

191

Barr, H. and O'Leary, E. (1966) *Probation Research: National Study of Probation. Trends and Regional Comparison in Probation (England and Wales). Home Office Study in the Causes of Delinquency and the Treatment of Offenders No. 8.* London: HMSO.

Bean, P. (1976) *Rehabilitation and Deviance.* London: Routledge & Kegan Paul.

Becker, H. (1967) 'Whose side are we on?' *Social Problems*, 14, 239–47.

Biestek, F. P. (1957) *The Casework Relationship.* London: George Allen & Unwin.

Bottoms, A. E. (1981) 'The Suspended Sentence in England, 1967–1978', *British Journal of Criminology*, 21, 1, 1–26.

Bottoms, A. E. and McWilliams, W. (1979) 'A Non-Treatment Paradigm for Probation Practice', *British Journal of Social Work*, 9, 2, 159–202.

Bottoms, A. E. and Sheffield, C. (1980) Unpublished Report to DHSS on Feasibility of Research into Intermediate Treatment.

Brewer, C. and Lait, J. (1980) *Can Social Work Survive?* London: Temple Smith.

Brody, S. R. (1976) *The Effectiveness of Sentencing. Home Office Research Study No. 35.* London: HMSO.

Bryant, M., Coker, J., Estlea, B., Himmel, S. and Knapp, T. (1978) 'Sentenced to Social Work', *Probation Journal*, 25, 4, 111–14.

Bulldog Report (1976) *Report on the First Year.* London: ILPAS.

Bulldog Report (1977) *Report on the Second Year.* London: ILPAS.

Bulldog Report (1980) *Report on the Fourth Year.* London: ILPAS.

Carlen, P. (1979) *Magistrates' Justice.* London: Martin Robertson.

Conference of Chief Probation Officers (1978) 'Sentencing is an Expression of Society's Attitudes towards Crime rather than a Method of Combating Recidivism'. Unpublished paper.

Croft, J. (1978) *Research in Criminal Justice. Home Office Research Study No. 44.* London: HMSO.

Curran, J. (1983) 'Social Enquiry Reports: A Selective Commentary on the Literature', in *Research Highlights No. 5. Social Work with Adult Offenders*, 44–59. University of Aberdeen, Department of Social Work.

Davies, M. (1974a) *Prisoners of Society: Attitudes and After Care.* London: Routledge & Kegan Paul.

Davies, M. (1974b) *Social Work in the Environment. Home Office Research Study No. 21.* London: HMSO.

Davies, M. (1979) 'Through the Eyes of the Probationer', *Probation Journal*, 26, 3, 84–8.

Davies, M. (1981) *The Essential Social Worker: A Guide to Positive Practice*. London: Heinemann.

Edwards, G. (1982) *The Treatment of Drinking Problems: A Guide for the Helping Professions*. New York: Grant McIntyre.

Evans, P. (1980) *Prison Crisis*. London: George Allen & Unwin.

Fairhead, S. (1981a) *Day Centres and Probation. Home Office Research Unit Paper No. 4*. London: HMSO.

Fairhead, S. (1981b) *Persistent Petty Offenders. Home Office Research Study No. 66*. London: HMSO.

Fairhead, S. and Marshall, T. F. (1979) 'Dealing with the Petty, Persistent Offender', in *The Petty Persistent Offender*, 1–9. London: NACRO.

Fineman, S. and Eden, C. (1979) 'Change within the Probation Service', *Personnel Review*, 8, 2, 30–5.

Fisher, A. (1978) 'Probation Service Exists on an Elaborate System of Pretence', *Social Work Today*, 9, 37, 16–18.

Fitzgerald, M. and Sim, J. (1979) *British Prisons*. Oxford: Blackwell.

Fitzmaurice, C. and Pease, K. (1982) 'Prison Sentences and Population: A Comparison of Some European Countries', *Justice of the Peace*, 146, 38, 575–9.

Folkard, M. S., Lyon, K., Carver, M. and O'Leary, E. (1966) *Probation Research: A Preliminary Report. Home Office Studies in the Causes of Delinquency and the Treatment of Offenders No. 7*. London: HMSO.

Folkard, M. S., Smith, D. E. and Smith D. D. (1976) *Impact. Intensive Matched Probation and After-Care Treatment; Volume 2, The Results of the Experiment. Home Office Research Study, No. 36*. London: HMSO.

Fullwood, C. (1976) 'Control in Probation, After-Care and Parole', in Control without Custody? Unpublished papers presented to the Cropwood Round Table Conference, December 1975.

Giller, H. and Morris, A. (1978) 'Supervision Orders: The Routinization of Treatment', *Howard Journal*, 17, 3, 149–59.

Greenberg, D. (1977) 'The Correctional Effect of Corrections: A Survey of Evaluations', in Greenberg, D. (ed.), *Corrections and Punishment; Sage Criminal Justice System Annuals, Vol. 8*. Beverly Hills: Sage.

194   BIBLIOGRAPHY

Griffiths, W. (1982a) 'A New Probation Service', *Probation Journal*, 29, 3, 98–9.

Griffiths, W. (1982b) 'Supervision in the Community', *Justice of the Peace*, 146, 35, 514–15.

Harré, R. and Secord, P. (1976) *The Explanation of Social Behaviour*. Oxford: Blackwell.

Harris, R. (1977) 'The Probation Officer as Social Worker', *British Journal of Social Work*, 7, 4, 433–42.

Harris, R. (1980) 'A Changing Service: The Case for Separating "Care" and "Control" in Probation Practice', *British Journal of Social Work*, 10, 3, 163–84.

Hil, R. (1980) Centre 81: A Study of the Genesis and Development of the Southampton Day Centre. Unpublished paper.

Hine, J. and McWilliams, W. (1981) 'Research Review No. 2: Social Inquiry Practice', *Probation Journal*, 38, 3, 93–7.

Hine, J., McWilliams, W. and Pease, K. (1978) 'Recommendations, Social Information and Sentencing', *Howard Journal*, 17, 2, 91–100.

Home Office (1969) *Report on the Work of the Probation and After-Care Department 1966–1968*. London: HMSO.

Home Office (1971) *Habitual Drunken Offenders: Report of the Working Party*. London: HMSO.

Home Office (1972) Working Party on the Use of Probation Resources. Unpublished paper.

Home Office (1977) *Review of Criminal Justice Policy 1976*. London: HMSO.

Home Office (1978a) 'A Survey of the South-East Prison Population'. *Home Office Research Bulletin No. 5*. London: Home Office.

Home Office (1978b) *The Sentence of the Court: A Handbook for Courts on the Treatment of Offenders*. London: HMSO.

Home Office (1979a) *Probation and After-Care Statistics England and Wales 1978*. London: Home Office.

Home Office (1979b) *Report of the Committee of Inquiry into the United Kingdom Prison Services*. London: HMSO.

Home Office (1979c) *Statistics of the Criminal Justice System England and Wales 1968–1978*. London: HMSO.

Home Office (1980a) *The Reduction of Pressure on the Prison System. Observations on the Fifteenth Report from the Expenditure Committee*. London: HMSO.

Home Office (1980b) *Statistics of the Criminal Justice System England and Wales 1969–1979*. London: HMSO.

Home Office (1981a) *Criminal Statistics England and Wales 1980*. London: HMSO.

Home Office (1981b) *Prison Statistics England and Wales 1980*. London: HMSO.

Home Office (1981c) *Probation and After-Care Statistics England and Wales 1980*. London: Home Office.

Home Office (1981d) *Report of Her Majesty's Chief Inspector of Prisons 1980*. London: HMSO.

Home Office (1981e) *Report on the Work of the Prison Department 1980*. London: HMSO.

Home Office (1981f) *Review of Parole in England and Wales*. London: HMSO.

Home Office (1982a) *Probation and After-Care Statistics England and Wales 1981*. London: Home Office.

Home Office (1982b) *Report on the Work of the Prison Department 1981*. London: HMSO.

Home Office (1983) *Report of Her Majesty's Chief Inspector of Prisons 1982*. London: HMSO.

Home Office (1984) *Criminal Justice: A Working Paper*. London: Home Office.

Hough, J. M. and Mayhew, P. (1983) *British Crime Survey. Home Office Research Study No. 76*. London: HMSO.

House of Commons (1978) *Fifteenth Report from the Expenditure Committee. The Reduction of Pressure on the Prison System*. London: HMSO.

Hunt, A. (1964) 'Enforcement in Probation Casework', *British Journal of Criminology*, 4, 3, 239–52.

Kessell, N. and Walton, H. (1965) *Alcoholism*. Harmondsworth: Penguin.

King, R. and Morgan, R. (1980) *The Future of the Prison System*. London: Gower.

Lacey, M., Pendleton, J. and Read, G. (1983) 'Supervision in the Community: The Righting of Wrongs', *Justice of the Peace*, 147, 8, 120–3.

Lipton, D., Martinson, R. and Wilks, J. (1975) *The Effectiveness of Correctional Treatment: A Survey of Treatment Evaluation Studies*. New York: Praeger.

McClintock, R. H. (1958) *The Results of Probation: A Report of the Cambridge Department of Criminal Science*. London: Macmillan.

McConville, S. (1981) *A History of English Prison Administration, 1750–1877, Vol. 1*. London: Routledge & Kegan Paul.

Medway Centre (1981) The Medway Centre Annual Report. Unpublished report, Kent Probation and After-care Service.

Meyer, J. and Timms, N. (1970) *The Client Speaks*. London: Routledge & Kegan Paul.

Millham, S. (1981) Report of Conference, Welsh IT Forum. Unpublished paper.

Morris, A., Giller, H., Szwed, E. and Geach, H. (1980) *Justice for Children*. London: Macmillan.

Morris, P. and Beverly, F. (1975) *On Licence: A Study of Parole*. London: Wiley.

Mott, J. (1977) 'Decision Making and Social Inquiry Reports In One Juvenile Court', *British Journal of Social Work*, 7, 4, 421–32.

Paley, J. and Thorpe, D. (1974) *Children: Handle with Care*. Leicester: National Youth Bureau.

Parliamentary All-Party Penal Affairs Group (1980) *Too Many Prisoners*. Chichester: Barry Rose.

Parliamentary All-Party Penal Affairs Group (1981) *Still Too Many Prisoners*. Chichester: Barry Rose.

Parsloe, P. (1976) 'Social Work and the Justice Model', *British Journal of Social Work*, 6, 1, 71–89.

Parsloe, P. (1979) 'Issues of Social Control', in King, J. F. S. (ed.), *Pressure and Change in the Probation Service. Cropwood Conference Series No. 11*. University of Cambridge, Institute of Criminology.

Payne, D. and Lawton, J. (1977) Day Training Centres. Unpublished Home Office report, London.

Pearson, G. (1983) *Hooliganism: A History of Respectable Fears*. London: Macmillan.

Pease, K. (1983) 'Penal Innovations', in *Research Highlights No. 5. Social Work with Adult Offenders*, 73–87. University of Aberdeen, Department of Social Work.

Pease, K., Billingham, S. and Earnshaw, I. (1977) *Community Service Assessed in 1976. Home Office Research Study No. 39*. London: HMSO.

Pease, K., Durkin, P., Earnshaw, I., Payne, D. and Thorpe, J. (1975) *Community Service Orders. Home Office Research Study No. 29*. London: HMSO.

Phillpotts, G. J. O. and Lancucki, L. B. (1979) *Previous Convictions, Sentence and Reconviction. Home Office Research Study No. 53.* London: HMSO.

Pointing, J. E. (1982) *Client Unemployment and Offending: The Bulldog Experiment.* London: ILPAS.

Priestley, P., McGuire, J., Flegg, D., Hemsley, V. and Welham, D. (1978) *Social Skills and Personal Problem Solving: A Handbook of Methods.* London: Tavistock.

Radzinowicz, L. (1958) Preface to McClintock, R. H., *The Results of Probation: A Report of the Cambridge Department of Criminal Science.* London: Macmillan.

Ragg, N. M. (1977) *People not Cases: A Philosophical Approach to Social Work.* London: Routledge & Kegan Paul.

Raison, T. (1980) *Under Age Drinking.* London: Home Office Press Release.

Rees, S. (1978) *Social Work Face to Face.* London: Edward Arnold.

Rutherford, A. (1984) The Massachusetts Alternative: A Radical Approach to Juvenile Justice, *The Listener*, 3 May, 2–4.

Scull, A. (1977) *Decarceration: Community Treatment and the Deviant – A Radical View.* Englewood Cliffs, New Jersey: Prentice-Hall.

Shaw, S. (1980) *Paying the Penalty: An Analysis of the Cost of Penal Sanctions.* London: NACRO.

Shearer, D. (1984) 'Citizen Participation in Local Government: A Critique and an Alternative Proposal', *International Journal of Urban and Regional Research*, 8, 4, 573–86.

Singer, L. R. (1980) 'Supportive Surveillance: Probation as Discipline', *International Journal of the Sociology of Law*, 8, 3, 251–75.

Smith, D. (1965) 'Front Line Organization of the State Mental Hospital', *Administrative Science Quarterly*, 10, 381–99.

Smith, G. (1979) *Social Work and the Sociology of Organizations.* London: Routledge & Kegan Paul.

Social Services Committee (1984) *Children in Care (Short Report). Second Report, Vol. 1.* London: HMSO.

Survey of Social Enquiry Reports (1980) Unpublished report, ILPAS.

Sussex, J. (1978) Medway Close Support Unit. Unpublished paper, Kent Probation and After-care Service.

Taylor, L. (1972) 'The Significance and Interpretation of Replies to Motivational Questions: The Case of Sex Offenders', *Sociology*, 6, 1, 23–40.

Taylor, L., Lacey, R. and Bracken, D. (1980) *In Whose Best Interests?* London: Cobden Trust/Mind.

Thorpe, D. (1978) 'Intermediate Treatment', in Tutt, N. (ed.), *Alternative Strategies for Coping with Crime.* Oxford: Blackwell.

Thorpe, D. (1983) 'Deinstitutionalization and Justice', in Morris, A. and Giller, H., *Providing Criminal Justice for Children.* London: Edward Arnold.

Thorpe, D., Smith, D., Green, C. and Paley, J. (1980) *Out of Care.* London: George Allen & Unwin.

Tulkens, H. (1979) *Some Developments in Penal Practice and Policy in Holland.* London: NACRO.

Tutt, N. S. (1976) 'Intermediate Treatment', *Social Work Service*, 11, 3–5.

Von Hirsch, A. (1976) *Doing Justice: The Choice of Punishments.* New York: Hill & Wang.

Walker, H. and Beaumont, B. (1981) *Probation Work: Critical Theory and Socialist Practice.* Oxford: Blackwell.

Watson, D. and Timms, N. (1978) *Philosophy in Social Work.* London: Routledge & Kegan Paul.

Whitfield, R. G. (1980) *The Role of Volunteers in the Penal System.* London: Howard League for Penal Reform.

Wildcat Report (1978) *The Wildcat Experiment: An Early Test of Supported Work.* New York: Vera Institute of Justice.

Willis, A. (1977) 'Community Service as an Alternative to Imprisonment: A Cautionary View', *Probation Journal*, 24, 4, 120–5.

Willis, A. (1979) Displacement from Custody. A Review of the Day Training Centre Experiment. Unpublished paper.

Willis, A. (1981a) 'Other Non-Custodial Measures', in Jones, H. (ed.), *Society Against Crime*, 218–54. Harmondsworth: Penguin.

Willis, A. (1981b) 'Prisons in Crisis', in Jones, H. (ed.), *Society Against Crime*, 158–92. Harmondsworth: Penguin.

Willis, A. (1981c) 'The Future of Corrections', in Jones, H. (ed.), *Society Against Crime*, 255–84. Harmondsworth: Penguin.

Wootton, B. (1959) *Social Science and Social Pathology.* London: George Allen & Unwin.

Notes on Contributors

Helen Bethune works as a freelance consultant and researcher, concerned with various kinds of addiction. She recently completed a book on addiction for self-help groups, *Off the Hook* (Methuen).

Ian Butler has been employed as a social worker for most of his career, specializing in Intermediate Treatment. He is currently Development Officer with the IT Fund.

Peter Harraway has worked as a probation officer and subsequently senior probation officer with ILPS. He has specialized in innovatory programmes, until recently as manager of the Demonstration Unit in North London.

Richard Hil was previously employed as Research and Information Officer with Hampshire Probation Service. He is currently Research Officer with Lambeth Social Services.

Patricia Maitland has been employed for the past eight years as Research Officer with ILPS.

Peter Murray has worked since 1980 as Research Officer for Kent Probation Service.

John Pointing was previously employed as a researcher and lecturer in housing and social policy, and subsequently as a probation researcher. After a short spell working for a government funding agency, he is now Assistant Director of the National Association of Victims Support Schemes.

Maurice Vanstone has worked as a probation officer and then senior probation officer in South Wales for several years. He has been Manager of Pontypridd Day Training Centre since 1976.

Andrew Willis has been a lecturer in Criminology at University of Wales, Cardiff, since 1976. He is also a member of the Council of the Howard League.

Index

201

13, 30–8, 51–2, 71, 90–1, 92–3,
106, 108, 109, 179–80, 188–9
in USA, 106–7, 180, 188
see also alternatives to custody,
custodial institutions, sentencing
practices
Powers of Criminal Courts Act, 1973,
31, 93
Prison Reform Trust, 4
prisons, *see* custodial institutions
probation officers, *see* social workers
probation orders
decline in use of, 29, 162–3, 164
flexibility of, 16, 55, 60–1, 68, 103–4,
179–80
use of in relation to alternatives to
custody, 21, 29, 30–8, 45, 55, 60,
68, 75, 91, 92–3, 97, 109, 162–3,
179–80, 181
see also social inquiry reports
probation service, *see* social work
(organization and management)
public opinion, 4–5, 23–4, 28, 37, 178,
190

reconviction rates, 19–20, 69, 80–1, 96,
111–12, 164
rehabilitation, 16, 50, 106–9, 126, 135,
136, 138, 176
see also social work
reoffending, 9–10, 13, 19, 37, 50, 69, 78,
80–1, 89, 92–3, 94, 96, 99–100,
104–5, 108, 112, 163–4
see also reconviction

sentencers
need for restrictions on powers of, 9,
21, 27, 30
punitive stance of, 7, 24, 30, 34, 35,
38, 133
support for non-custodial penalties,
33, 58–9, 65
sentencing practices, 7–9, 10, 20–1,
27–36, 56–61, 68, 94–5, 163, 183
government position on, 9, 20, 27–9,
30, 32–3, 38
punitive trend of, 7–8, 22, 25, 38, 57
see also social inquiry reports

social control, 2, 38, 42, 52, 74, 121,
162, 167, 175, 176, 177, 178–80
social inquiry reports, 27, 30–8, 56,
57–8, 61, 62, 65, 68–9, 75, 95, 166,
186, 189
social work
and community-based programmes,
12, 37, 56, 72–3, 127–8, 135–6,
139
methods, 10, 11–15, 42–4, 62–8, 73,
75, 79, 83–90, 93–4, 101, 102–5,
109, 125–6, 135, 139, 146–8, 161,
167–70, 183, 187
and 'non-treatment paradigm', 12,
15–16, 75, 77, 88, 90, 105, 148,
162, 164–5, 168–76, 177–9, 181
organization and management, 7, 8,
10, 13, 44, 73–6, 84, 89, 107–9,
126, 180–1, 183–6, 189
theory, 10, 12, 113, 148, 166, 183,
185, 186
see also offending, penal policy,
probation orders, social inquiry
reports
social work clients
and choice, 15, 63, 76–7, 87, 102–4,
105, 147, 178, 181
dependency on programmes, 43–4,
87, 138, 161
perceptions of self, 66, 79, 97,
99–100, 102, 105, 119, 122,
123–5, 138, 145, 152–6, 159, 169
perceptions of social work, 10–11,
11–12, 13, 17, 102, 104, 112–13,
125, 162, 165–6, 170–6, 186
perceptions of social workers, 48–50,
77–9, 82, 101, 120–1, 122, 156,
160, 174–6
unemployment amongst, 14, 75,
81–3, 85, 89, 91, 98–9, 108,
113–14, 117–18, 122–8,
168, 171, 174, 177
see also alternatives to custody,
offenders, offending
social workers
and client control, 12, 40–3, 51–3,
76–7, 88, 126, 164, 167, 170, 176,
179–80, 190